NOCTURNE
THE OFFICIAL STRATEGY GUIDE

Gathering of Developers, Ltd.

Dallas, Texas

www.godgames.com

www.marspub.com

Edwin E. Steussy, Publisher
Amy Yancey, Coodination and Design
Michael Duggan, Graphic Artist

Contents

THE OFFICIAL STRATEGY GUIDE

NOCTURNE

NOCTURNE
Official Strategy Guide

Chapter One – Introduction & Game Basics

THE OFFICIAL STRATEGY GUIDE

Nocturne, in simple terms, is a third-person, action adventure which takes place in the late 1920s to early 1940s. However, Nocturne is anything but simple. Drawing upon elements from classic horror, most notably H.P. Lovecraft, and melding them with gritty, no-nonsense detective work (a la Sam Spade), Nocturne delivers a visceral combination never before seen in computer gaming.

The game is divided into four Acts, or chapters. They are playable in any order, and chronicle the adventures of The Spookhouse, a top-secret government agency chartered with ridding the world of supernatural forces bent on human destruction. More specifically, the player takes on the role of The Stranger, a dark, enigmatic figure who stalks monsters relentlessly.

As the Stranger, you'll travel the world, from 1920s Germany, to France in 1935, seeking out evil and destroying it. Encountering one fiendish foe after another, your goal is to rid the world of every supernatural being bent on destroying the human race. This guide is intended to help when you're stuck and can't go any further on your own. While you can certainly use it to go through the game step-by-step, doing so will severely impact your enjoyment of the game. There are many surprises in store for you in Nocturne; try to experience them as they were intended first. You can always look here for the answers when you need them.

In this book you'll find:

Chapter 1: Game Basics—An overview of the game, including strategies and tips for making it through in one piece.

Chapter 2: Heroes and Villains—The cast of characters, both good and evil, that you will encounter in your travels.

Chapter 3: Bestiary—A rundown of the monsters known to Spookhouse, including the best way to defeat them.

Chapter 4: Gear—Everything, including weapons and health, the Stranger will need to complete the missions.

Chapters 5-9: Walkthroughs—Detailed, step-by-step instructions for making it through each mission, including dialog from the actual script that the developers used to design the game.

NOCTURNE

CHAPTER ONE: INTRODUCTION & GAME BASICS

Game Basics

If you've read the Nocturne game manual cover-to-cover, you've got a good head start. If, like most people, you ripped open the game box, plugged the CD in, and didn't bother much with the manual, you're still in good shape, since you have a general idea of how the program works.The following pages contain a quick overview of getting around in Nocturne. While we won't tell you how to use all the in-game menus, you will find out how to set things up properly, and learn a few tricks that will make it much easier for you to survive.

Getting Started

There are a few things you can do before you even start the game to make your life easier. Although you don't have to do these things, you should take a close look at your setup before you dive in. It will save you plenty of frustration.

Adjust your gamma setting

First, when you are prompted to calibrate your monitor, you'll be guided through the process of setting it up. Chances are that when you start playing, everything will be very dark—sinister and scary, to be sure, but if you calibrated it as instructed, you will have a hard time seeing anything until it's too close to do anything about. Use F11 to brighten things up a bit, and it will definitely make things easier. Don't crank the gamma all the way down to .5 (it's the lowest setting, which corresponds to a bright-as-day look), or you'll completely ruin the atmosphere of the game.

Check your detail levels

Sound and graphic detail can seriously impact Nocturne gameplay on some machines. Unless you are running a Pentium III 450 or better, with 256Mb of RAM, don't maximize the settings in either the Graphic Options, or Sound Options menus. Start with a medium level of graphic detail, and a reasonable sound setup. If things work well, then you can consider increasing one or both later.

Use the advantages built into the game

Setting your aiming to AUTO-AIM is not a crutch; if you use the pistols, it's the only way to target more than one enemy at a time. Likewise, set your health usage to AUTO, so that Stranger will use health automatically. Most monsters incapacitate you for a few seconds while they bite/attack. If you don't have health set to AUTO, you'll be helpless until the attack is over, or until you can fight back.

THE OFFICIAL STRATEGY GUIDE

Save your game often

There are no penalties for saving the game often. Save before any difficult maneuver, or when you've just completed a tough segment. Nothing is worse than dying and having to redo a large section of the game because you forgot to save. Get in the habit of using F2 to save.

Controlling The Stranger

The control setup for Nocturne is fairly intuitive—you should be able to customize your controls in a matter of moments. However, setting your controls up and using them effectively are two different things.

Getting used to movement

Unfortunately, the Stranger can't slowly make his way through each of the missions. You need to learn how to quickly make him do what you want him to do, but at first, your results may not be what you'd like. The best thing you can do is play around with him; you will have control of him in Spookhouse HQ long before you ever begin a mission. Walk around—run, jump, draw your weapons, push light switches, and talk to everyone. The sooner you get a feel for what the Stranger can (and can't) do, the easier it will be to tackle the missions.

Pay special attention to moving when the Stranger is facing you. This is a particularly difficult task the first few times you try it, but you will have to perform it often, as the camera angles in the game will sometimes force you to do so. A good rule of thumb is, if you aren't sure which way he will move when you press a key, don't press it. Think it through before you move.

Lining up for jumps

One of the trickiest moves the Stranger will have to perform is a jump from one platform to the next. Until you get used to jumping, draw your pistols (or another weapon that has an aiming sight) and point them down at the platform to which you're jumping. If they are lined up with your destination, then the Stranger is lined up straight for his jump. Walk to the edge of the platform and make the leap. In most cases, a standing jump is enough to get you there, so try that first (after you save your game).

NOCTURNE

CHAPTER ONE: INTRODUCTION & GAME BASICS

Using camera angles

The static cameras in Nocturne can occasionally cause some problems, since your view will switch as the Stranger enters another camera's zone. For this reason, NEVER rush from camera view to camera view without pausing slightly until your view adjusts. You never know what's on the other side until you get there, so keep a weapon drawn and move cautiously into new areas. There are many cases where by inching close to a camera transition, you can trigger the switch to another view before actually entering the area. This is very useful for jumps or for entering areas you know to be swarming with monsters.

Death isn't always so bad

If you're not sure if the Stranger can perform an action, save your game and try it. If it works, life is good. If not, then restore your game and try it again. You can survive anything if you use this method throughout the game. Many times, the Stranger will reveal something to you as he dies, by falling past an area you hadn't noticed, or something similar. So don't be afraid to kill him off once in awhile, especially if you're not sure how to get past an area.

Hand-to-hand combat

It's not documented in the manual, but the Stranger does have limited hand-to-hand fighting skills. If under attack before you can draw a weapon, use the action/attack key to swing at a monster as soon as possible. If the attacker is behind the Stranger, use the BACK key to deliver a backward kick that may loosen an attacker's grip. Needless to say, if you're reduced to this form of combat, your goal is to get away and draw a weapon. If you're attacked while holding a shotgun or other powerful weapon in your hand, and the attacker is behind you, you can still blast your way loose; the recoil from a shotgun blast will knock a monster off the Stranger's back, allowing you to bring your weapon to bear and finish the job.

Puzzle Solving

Nocturne includes several diabolical puzzles that the Stranger will be forced to solve in order to continue. Although the solutions to these puzzles are in this guide, there are still a few things you can do to increase your chances of solving a puzzle. Keep in mind that a locked door is a puzzle with an obvious solution—a key.

NOCTURNE

THE OFFICIAL STRATEGY GUIDE

Save often

As mentioned above, save your game as soon as you encounter a puzzle, and be sure to use a different name for each saved game. That way, you can restore from wherever you were if your puzzle attempt fails.

Try the obvious first

In many cases, if something looks like it will work, it will. Give it a shot (after you've saved your game).

Use your inventory

Anything the Stranger can pick up may be useful for a puzzle. There are very few cases where an item you can put in inventory won't be useful later on. Be a pack rat and collect everything you can.

General Tips

Following are a few more tips that come from many hours of gameplay. They should allow you to avoid some of the hazards of monster hunting and help you gather information as well.

Talk to everyone: You never know who might have information that will help in a mission.

Monsters are never friendly: Shoot first when it comes to monsters; hesitation will kill the Stranger quickly.

Run!: In many cases, your best defense is to run away faster than the monsters chasing you. Ammunition can be scarce, so don't be afraid to move it when necessary.

Protect your companions: If you're with someone, or escorting a citizen to safety, protect them by placing Stranger between them and danger. Monsters will exploit defenselessness; don't give them the chance.

Be suspicious: Friendly characters may be monsters in disguise, or have diabolical plans for the Stranger.

NOCTURNE

NOCTURNE
Official Strategy Guide

Chapter Two – Heroes & Villains

THE OFFICIAL STRATEGY GUIDE

There are several key characters, both good and bad, in Nocturne. This chapter gives you some information about them, and in the case of the villains, tells you how to defeat them.

Warning: This chapter contains "spoilers," or information about the game that will spoil some of the plot surprises in the game. Don't read this chapter if you'd rather discover them on your own.

Heroes

The Stranger

In 1923, Spookhouse accepted (under still-classified circumstances) the enlistment of a mysterious man without identity or history. The man rose almost immediately through the loose ranks of the officially nonexistent agency. He is considered one of the most valuable Spookhouse operatives. Though certainly not superhuman, the man's prowess inspires an excess of whispered rumors. But those rumors remain in the realm of speculation. Unflappable, and unmovable, the Stranger is expressionless and stoic. His deep, rough voice is quiet and reserved, and he speaks only when necessary.

NOCTURNE

CHAPTER TWO: HEROES & VILLAINS

Elspeth "Doc" Holliday

Professor Elspeth Holliday is an undisputed genius in the fields of applied science and mechanical engineering. Many of her more conservative colleagues have branded her a dangerous, radical eccentric. She insists on testing her own fantastic inventions in the field. Doc Holliday asserts that she hasn't the time for rigorous laboratory testing. Some whisper that she can't stand still long enough. Doc Holiday is a scientist, an adventurer, a monster-hunter. She concentrates on accomplishing her objectives with such narrow focus that she tends to neglect social conventions and niceties. She expects and requires a great deal from herself and others and is not particularly charitable to weakness.

Hiram Mottra

Hiram's service to Spookhouse consists mainly of research and documentation. Occasionally, he is called upon to go into the field in a combat capacity, but his nervous nature and considerable bulk make him ill-equipped as a soldier. To compensate, he tends to carry an assortment of silver, wood, and mercury weapons so that he can handle confrontations with practically any supernatural creature. His education included a small amount of medical training, so his services as a medic are sometimes employed.

He reportedly possesses the ability to use an unproven, extra sense that allows him to "feel" aggressive thoughts directed at him. Some think this "sixth sense" is actually just paranoia, but more often than not, his feelings prove true. Speaking in hushed, frightened tones, Hiram seems almost always on the edge of fright.

Colonel Cedric Feldspar Hapscomb

Colonel Hapscomb was one of the last Great White Hunters of India in the waning days of Britannia's rule. Originally a military officer stationed in Bombay, he was sickened by the injustices perpetrated on the native people by his army and the Indian government. He spent any off-duty time comforting the downtrodden. He led many safaris into the Indian bush, and his reputation as a good man and a great hunter spread among the Indian natives. The great cities, however, were encroaching on the wide-open wild that he loved, and he was growing bored. He had tracked and bagged all the great beasts on the continent. He turned his attention to whispered reports of monsters stalking the countryside in India and abroad. He served as an honorary liaison for Spookhouse in its early years, and was made a full agent when its charter expanded and the head of field operations, Marlon Lepus, retired.

Svetlana Lupescu (Dhampir)

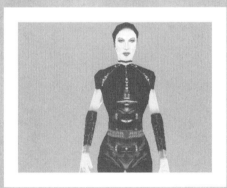

Svetlana was born from the union of a vampire father and human mother. Her mother, as is almost always the case, died in childbirth. She has never met her father. Dreaded and shunned by her mother's wealthy family and by the small community into which she was born, a kindly household servant spirited her away and carried her to the United States, where she deposited her in the care of Spookhouse agents. The predatory nature and (albeit faint) nocturnal powers of Svetlana's vampiric side perfectly complement her human loathing of vampires. Svetlana has developed into a hunter with unparalleled potential, but the truth of her origin and the clinical sterility of her upbringing has left her somewhat distanced from other team members.

NOCTURNE

CHAPTER TWO: HEROES & VILLAINS

Scat Dazzle

Scat Dazzle was born deep in the Louisiana bayous. He was marked as a special child, a magic child, in the small, voodoo-worshipping community in which he was raised. He was groomed to be a powerful houngan, or voodoo priest, from very early childhood. The practiced mambas and houngans dedicated him to the service of Baron Samedi, a powerful voodoo Loa, a sort of god, when he grew into maturity and power. On Dazzle's eighteenth birthday, Baron

Samedi violently seized control of Dazzle's body during an onstage jazz performance and forced him to flee the speak-easy in which he was playing, which was firebombed by racketeers immediately afterward. The club burned to the ground. There were no other survivors. Eventually, Dazzle gained enough control of his faculties to resist Baron Samedi's total control. Their two personalities began to merge somewhat, and now each has some control over the other. Dazzle can summon the Baron at will, but depending on his strength level, cannot always control him.

Baron Samedi

Although sometimes referred to as gods for simplicity's sake, Loa are actually the immortal, archetypal representations of the natural world and of moral principles, such as the ocean, death, war, and love. Baron Samedi is the most powerful member of the Guédé family, and the Loa who represents death. He tells lewd jokes, makes obscene gestures, smokes cigarettes, eats voraciously, and drinks rum. Extremely cocky and proud, the Baron can do things no man can do, but he only responds to requests for help if doing so pleases his chaotic moods.

THE OFFICIAL STRATEGY GUIDE

Vincenzo "Icepick" Gasparro

Originally an enforcer for the Ghiberti Family in Chicago, Icepick was betrayed and "sold" to Professor Loathring as an early experiment in Capone's "Frankenmob" scheme. Already a large man, experimental medical procedures transformed him into a giant. Horribly scarred and stitched together, Gasparro was found and "turned" to Spookhouse service by Doc Holliday. To this day, he displays fanatical loyalty and protectiveness towards her.

Moloch (demon)

Like many of his fellow Spookhouse operatives, Moloch is an outcast. During the Nepalese Horucide of 1921, Moloch fought alongside the Spookhouse agents. While not allied with Spookhouse, Moloch shared a common enemy: the demon underworld that had cast him out of hell centuries before. He assisted in the sealing of the portal in the mountains of Nepal, and Spookhouse brought him back to America afterwards to consider him as a potential agent.

His presence at Spookhouse proved intolerable to some of the older members. They saw his monstrous presence as an abomination of the charter of Spookhouse. Several fled the organization in disgust, including the top monster hunter at the time, Hamilton Killian.

NOCTURNE

CHAPTER TWO: HEROES & VILLAINS

General Seymore Biggs

General Biggs is a general through and through. He comes from a family tradition of military service. He has been a member of the armed forces for his entire life and would have it no other way. Throughout his military career, he has moved up in rank at an amazing rate, proving himself as the ideal soldier, willing to sacrifice everything if it meant the United States would benefit. More than that, his military genius is undeniable.

A few years after becoming a General in 1929, Biggs met Colonel Hapscomb. They have become close friends since, and in 1933, General Biggs was officially brought on as an outside Spookhouse "agent" in charge of gathering regular troops that will act as cover for Spookhouse, and later deny any existence of supernatural activity.

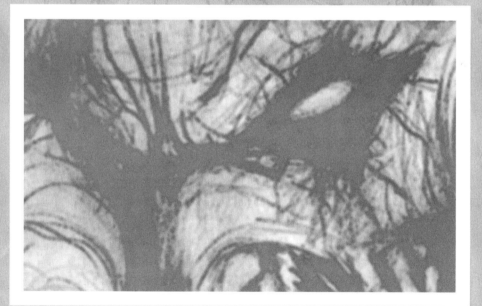

Villains

Alpha Werewolf

(Leader of the Hökkendire Werewolf Tribe)

One of the few survivors of the Hökkendire Werewolf Horucide of 1924 (which the Stranger led), the Alpha has rebuilt his tribe and now seeks out those who had so nearly killed him and his people.

NOCTURNE

CHAPTER TWO: HEROES & VILLAINS

Count Voicu (Vampire Master)

Voicu is the master vampire residing in castle Gaustadt and reigns over the village Falkenburg. Through several hundred years of dominating the world around him, Voicu's voice, thick with a German accent originating in the Middle Ages, and demeanor are that of a powerful master of his domain.

The count can be killed by a wooden stake through his heart, but it's unlikely that the Stranger will get that chance. The best way to kill the Count is to use the Holy Relic found in the chapel inside the castle walls. A few solid strikes with it, and Voicu will be destroyed.

Hamilton Killian

(Retired Spookhouse Operative)

After the death of his wife at the hands of a vampire, Killian's heart turned to fire, and an unrelenting hatred of monsters boiled inside him. He served Spookhouse for a few years, gradually becoming less and less stable. His retirement was only partially voluntary.

Having fought alongside his countryman Colonel Hapscomb, Killian commands the same sort of authoritative British voice. As he descended into madness, that powerful voice becomes more and more frightening.

Killian is not a good guy—he captures the Stranger and forces him through a maze meant to kill him. Needless to say, when Killian's death comes, the Stranger is not unhappy to see him go.

NOCTURNE

CHAPTER TWO: HEROES & VILLAINS

Priest of Gardath (Black Magician)

Having studied from the dread Necronomicon and other forbidden texts, the Priest (whose name was once Martin before he changed it to Martinus and then discarded such mundane things as names from his life) has found the prison of one of the elder gods under the plains of West Texas.

You won't have to fight this villain; Gardath has become displeased with him and will do the job for you.

Smiley

The biggest, toughest Frankenmobster under Capone's command, Smiley is a monster who relentlessly stalks the Stranger in Chicago. Smiley remembers his days as a simple Mafia goon. He rose to become the most powerful, and through the medical ministrations of the vile Doctor Loathring, he exceeds all human capabilities.

You'll face Smiley three times in Act 3—once in the theater, again in the warehouse, and finally in the factory. Each time, he has been noticeably patched together by Capone's doctors, and he is stronger than his previous incarnation. The first time you meet him, use the Elephant Gun to take him down. In the warehouse, the Flamethrower is the best way to bring him down. To kill him once and for all, shoot the catwalk support he's standing on in the factory, and he'll be dumped into a vat of corrosive chemicals to die for good.

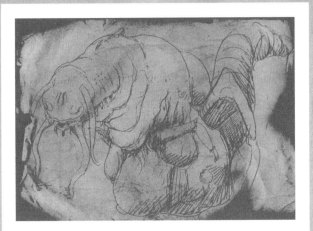

NOCTURNE
Official Strategy Guide

Chapter Three - Bestiary

THE OFFICIAL STRATEGY GUIDE

Spookhouse has catalogued many different monsters using data gathered during its numerous operations. The following is a brief summary of the most prevalent monsters they've encountered, as well as some they know to exist, but have little current information about.

Drones / Larvae

Description: In aeons past, in a time before man rose to power, other ancient races ruled this planet. Now, few traces of their heritage remains. One such vestigial remnant of that nameless race is a sub-species that might have preceded modern insects. Forming a society not unlike a bee hive, these creatures go through a remarkable life cycle. Born as slug-like larvae, the creatures develop into bipedal multi-armed drones of hideous proportions. Their purpose is to protect their queen.

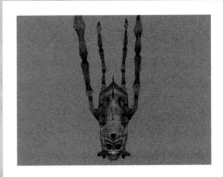

Neutralization: Use a shotgun, or other assault weapon at close range. Alternately, you can use explosives if available. Drones have no long-range attacks, but Larvae can toss acid-like projectiles. Be prepared to use explosives on large groups of Larvae in order to avoid serious injury.

Gargoyles

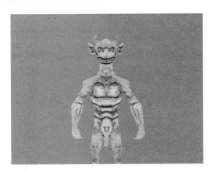

Description: No written records have survived the centuries to explain the original intent of the grotesque forms of the stone gargoyles. In these modern time, gargoyles are considered little more than decoration, but from deep in their past, their true nature remains. By carving the visage of evil upon stone, man has invited that evil to enter the stone. When demons inhabit the art of man, the results can terrify, allowing the stone to live.

NOCTURNE

CHAPTER THREE: BESTIARY

Neutralization: Gargoyles are only animate when unseen; as soon as they come into your field of vision, they become stone once again, and cannot be killed in that form. Killing a Gargoyle is an elaborate game of cat and mouse, since you must turn away long enough for them to move, then spin quickly around and blast them with your weapon. They are vulnerable to just about any projectile weapon when in their animated state.

Ghouls

Description: From the darkest depths of evil, Ghouls rise to deliver terrifying destruction to mankind. Their bestial forms are virtually immune to damage, and no mere mortal can hope to kill them permanently. Possessing dark intelligence, Ghouls attack quickly and lethally, shrugging off wounds that would stop any natural creature. They know that humans fear them utterly, and they enjoy the terror they inspire.

Neutralization: Ghouls are some of the toughest creatures to kill, because as long as they are capable, they will rise and continue to attack. Blessed weapons are the only sure way to put a Ghoul down for good, but they can also be stopped if you can manage to dismember them completely with a blade or firearm. They can't rise if half of their body is missing, so this is sometimes the default way of killing Ghouls, since blessed weapons are somewhat rare.

Imps

Description: More pesky than dangerous, imps are the snickering cousins of gremlins. The squat, red creatures revel in causing havoc and disturbing otherwise peaceful people. Rising from the grey pits surrounding hell, imps seek out and torment hapless victims. Sometimes their actions prove hazardous, but usually they merely annoy and frighten.

NOCTURNE

THE OFFICIAL STRATEGY GUIDE

Neutralization: Imps are very pesky, and in groups, they can be deadly. However, a solid blast with a shotgun or other assault weapon usually takes care of them. Imps are rarely found alone, so if you see one, keep a sharp eye out for its brothers who are likely to be sneaking up behind you.

Mobsters

Description: Normally, members of the Mafia would not be referred to as "monsters." But once they've been shredded by a tommygun, re-assembled and re-animated, these franken-mobsters no longer qualify as humans. The result of a lifetime of research by Doctor Enric Loathring, these undead hitmen served Al Capone during the waning days of Prohibition.

Neuralization: Re-animated goons can be killed with just about any weapon, but since most of them carry Tommyguns, you'll need to kill them with something that has decent range. Be sure to grab their Tommyguns after they are dead—they won't be needing them, but you will

Sentinels

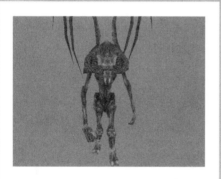

Description: Summoned from a darker realm, sentinels are the tools of one who masters great power. These massive, winged fiends can be sent anywhere to do the bidding of their master. Their shape is hideous, their odor foul, and the leathery flapping of their wings drives men mad with fear.

Neutralization: Sentinels are tough to bring down with pistols, but it can be done. One benefit to using pistols is their auto-aim feature, which allows you to target the Sentinels as they hover overhead. However, don't get fancy; kill these hellish creatures with a shotgun blast as soon as possible.

NOCTURNE

CHAPTER THREE: BESTIARY

Skeletons

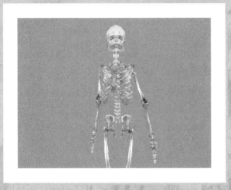

Description: Sometimes the dead simply do not stay still. In some cases, they become zombies, but their flesh eventually rots away. Those bodies raised by the darkest evil will continue to function regardless of the absence of muscle and flesh. Driven by spirits summoned from the darker realms, these bodies will eventually decay into bare skeletons. They can be shattered, but the forces holding them together will eventually collect the parts into a whole again.

Neutralization: You can't destroy Skeletons. In fact, the more you kill them, the faster they regenerate. The best thing to do when faced with these monsters is to keep moving—if they can't keep up, they'll forget about you. If they are following you too closely, lead them away and come back to give them the slip. If you simply must shoot them, use a shotgun at close range, then relocate before they reconstruct.

Succubus

Description: Succubi are diabolical female demons who ensnare men with supernatural beauty and hypnotic eyes. Any man too weak to avoid their temptation is drained of his blood and life essence. But even men with enough resolve to flee can rarely escape once the succubus shows her true, demonic form.

Neutralization: If one can't avoid looking at them, there is a very great chance that males will be ensnared by their dark charms. Although easily dispatched with most weapons, most men caught in a Succubus's stare don't have the desire to fire a single shot. For this reason, immediately shoot any Succubus on sight—don't give it the chance to lure you in.

NOCTURNE

Vampires

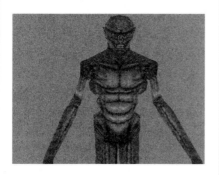

Description: Perhaps one of the most ancient of monster myths is that of the vampire, creatures that subsist on the living blood of human victims. Along with superhuman strength and the ability to transform into a variety of forms, vampires seduce their victims with powerful hypnotic forces. Stunned once the monster has penetrated their minds, the hapless victims cannot flee

Neutralization: A wooden stake or crossbow bolt through the heart is the only way to kill a Vampire. Aqua Vampira, Spookhouse's holy water formula, is also very effective when used in bullets. Of course, all Vampires are vulnerable to sunlight as well.

Vampire Brides

Description: When a vampire chooses, he can take a woman as his bride. He takes her blood and replaces it with his own. The woman becomes a vampire, and her mind is linked directly to her master's. She becomes his obedient servant and toy. To protect him, she will fight to the death, using the charms of her immortal beauty to lure unwary men to their deaths.

Neutralization: Vampire Brides have the same limitations as Vampires and can be killed in the same way. Unlike Vampires, they tend to fly much of the time in their humanoid form, making them difficult targets. Their incessant murmuring makes them easy to track down. Show no mercy—although they are beautiful, they are some of the deadliest creatures in the undead realm.

NOCTURNE

CHAPTER THREE: BESTIARY

Werewolves

Description: These creatures from legend have existed for thousands of years. The origin of the werewolf is shrouded in myth and speculation. Once human, these beasts have acquired the essence of the wolf which causes them to transform into half-human, half-wolf creatures capable of feats of fantastic strength and speed. Large tribes still roam the country-side in Europe, Asia, and Africa.

Neutralization: Silver bullets are the time-honored way to kill Werewolves, but they can also be killed by normal bullets and shells. It simply takes many more to bring them down. It is very rare for a Werewolf to travel alone, as they usually travel in packs or tribes, so that they can easily overwhelm their prey.

Zombies

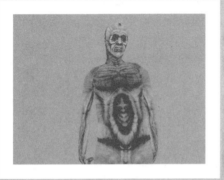

Description: They once walked the earth as normal human beings, and they died as all men must die. But for these soulless creatures, death could not contain them. They rose from their graves and now walk the earth as undead zombies. Summoned by powers beyond mortal comprehension, zombies exist only to feed on the flesh of the living. They wander mindless and unfocused.

Neutralization: Type I Zombies are easily dispatched by Voodoo magic, but unfortunately, these are not the only type of Zombies that exist. Others must be blown apart or have their heads removed in order to remove the evil force that animates their dead brains. Zombies are little threat to an armed opponent, unless they have the element of surprise. Once down, they usually stay down.

NOCTURNE

NOCTURNE
Official Strategy Guide

Chapter Four - Gear

THE OFFICIAL STRATEGY GUIDE

Throughout the four Acts, the Stranger will be able to use various items, including five weapon types, various health restoratives, keys, and other valuable items. The Stranger will find items that can be used directly (such as weapons and health), or items that must be used on something else (such as keys or ammo for weapons).

Weapons

The Stranger's weapons are grouped into five categories that are accessed by the weapons keys (1-5) on your keyboard. When you select a weapon category, use the NEXT WEAPON key (default key is =) to cycle through the available weapons in that category. If you are currently out of ammunition for a weapon, it will appear in the list, but won't be available until you have ammo for it.

Many of the weapons the Stranger can wield are intended for specific monsters, so it's important that you use the right weapon for the job.

Loading/selecting ammo

Each weapon may have more than one type of ammunition that can be loaded into it. As an example, the .45 pistols can be loaded with Silver bullets or regular .45 bullets. Use the LOAD AMMO key (default key is /) to toggle between the types of ammunition you are carrying.

NOCTURNE

CHAPTER FOUR: GEAR

Pistol Weapons

Pistol weapons are held in each of the Stranger's hands and can be fired separately at their targets. The only pistol weapons in Nocturne are the .45 Pistols.

45 Pistols - The Stranger's weapons of choice. These powerful handguns lay down a barrage that's deadly to most of the monsters you'll encounter. If used with Aiming set to AUTOMATIC, each pistol can track a different target, allowing the Stranger to fire on two targets at once. The pistols are aimed by using a special Ectoplasmic targeting system designed by Doc Holliday, which will track only undead targets. This safety feature keeps the Stranger fromshooting human targets.

Lethal against: Zombies, Werewolves (Silver Bullets), Vampires (Aqua Vampira), Sentinels, Imps, Demons (Mercury Bullets), Drones/Larvae, and Succubi.

Assault Weapons

Assault weapons pack more punch than the Stranger's twin .45's. The Shotgun and Tommygun will thin a crowd of monsters quickly, while the Crossbow and Elephant gun are the ultimate tools for dropping vampires and tough targets respectively. Assault weapons require the Stranger to use both hands to fire them, and can only be aimed at one target at a time.

Shotgun - The Shotgun is an extremely powerful short-range weapon. The green cone of damage that extends from the barrel shows the blast area of the shotgun. Aim it at approaching monsters to target them. Monsters closer to the Stranger will take more damage than those farther away. A head shot at close range with this weapon will usually do the trick.

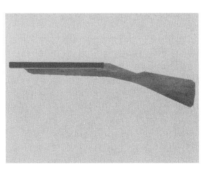

Lethal against: Zombies, Werewolves, Imps, Ghouls (temporarily), Sentinels, Drones/Larvae, and Succubi.

Thompson sub-machinegun (aka Tommygun) - Preferred weapon of Al Capone's mob. This rapid-fire machinegun will perforate a target in short order, and is the ultimate tool for clearing a room full of unwelcome guests.

Lethal against: You'll only get the chance to use it against re-animated gangsters, and it does a nice job of killing them. Again.

Crossbow - The Crossbow is especially designed to kill vampires. It fires wooden bolts in a gattling gun configuration, which makes it a perfect tool for the job. One shot to the heart with this weapon will drop most blood-suckers to the dirt.

Lethal against: Vampires, Vampire Brides, and Ghouls (Blessed bolts)

NOCTURNE

CHAPTER FOUR: GEAR

Elephant gun - This powerful rifle is designed to fire a high-caliber slug at the target. One shot from the Elephant gun is powerful enough to blast limbs from monsters, which enables the Stranger to incapacitate even the most powerful of foes.

Lethal against: Nearly everything; however, you'll only get to use it against Capone's undead army. One shot can easily destroy the average Frankenmobster.

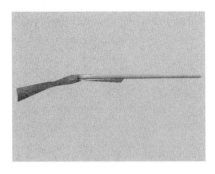

Flame Weapons

Flame weapons allow the Stranger to incinerate monsters. These weapons will continue to damage targets after initial contact, eventually destroying them. Fuel for Flame weapons is difficult to find, so use them sparingly. Some monsters can only be killed by using these weapons, so save fuel for them.

Flamethrower - The Flamethrower fires a stream of a gasoline mixture that is ignited by a flame near the end of the barrel. This liquid stream of fire coats targets and inflicts massive burning damage. It can be used on multiple targets, making it extremely useful for clearing crowded areas.

Lethal against: Frankenmobsters. Be very careful, as this is one of the few weapons that can harm the Stranger himself.

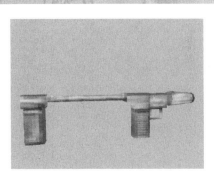

NOCTURNE

Sun of God (sunlight emitter) - This experimental weapon fires a burst of concentrated artificial sunlight at a target. This weapon is tailor-made for vampire killing, or for use against any other night creature that is sensitive to sunlight.

Lethal against: Vampires, Vampire Brides

Grenade Weapons

Grenade weapons are the Stranger's weapons of mass destruction. The powerful blasts from this category of weapons will obliterate anything unfortunate enough to be too close to the detonation point, including the Stranger, if you're not careful.

Dynamite - Good old-fashioned blasting sticks. When you light the fuse, the Stranger has only a few seconds to toss the dynamite away from him. Hold down the ACTION, or fire key, and you'll see an aiming arc that lengthens as you continue to hold it down. When it reaches the area you want to hit, release it, and the Stranger will throw it. Don't hold it too long, or throw it too close, or you'll completely erase the Stranger when the dynamite blows.

Lethal against: All but the most poweful undead creatures (Vampire Brides, Vampires, and Demons)

CHAPTER FOUR: GEAR

Melee Weapons

The final weapon category is melee, or hand-to-hand weapons. These are the Stranger's last resort, but that doesn't make them useless. Melee weapons can be used to break down doors and perform other tasks in addition to killing monsters.

Ax - This is a very basic weapon that can still have a decent effect on some monsters, such as Zombies. With proper aim, the Stranger can lop arms, heads, or other body parts from attackers. However, the short range of an axe makes it a weapon to be used only out of desperation. Use it as a tool first, and a weapon second.

Lethal against: Zombies

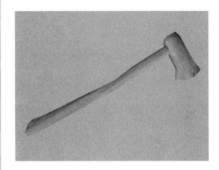

Bladed Weapon - A fierce-looking bladed weapon good for slashing monsters and chopping limbs off in the process.

Lethal against: Zombies, Ghouls

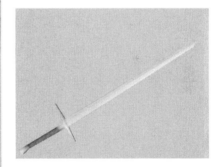

Holy Relic - A bladed relic of holy design. Powerful against undead, such as Vampires.

Lethal against: Vampires, especially Count Voicu. This is the weapon of his downfall.

Shovel - More useful as a weapon than a digging tool, but it's not very useful as a weapon. The only advantage it has over an axe is its reach, which will keep Zombies at bay longer.

Lethal against: Nothing, but can be used in a pinch to finish off Zombies.

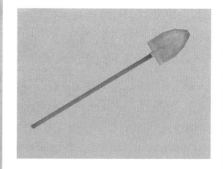

Wooden stake - Typically used for killing vampires. Getting close enough to use this takes serious nerve.

Lethal against: Vampires, Vampire Brides

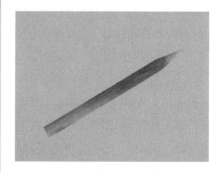

NOCTURNE

CHAPTER FOUR: GEAR

Ammunition

Some of the Stranger's weapons require ammunition to work, but many of these weapons can be loaded with different types of ammunition as well.

Bullets - Ammunition for the Stranger's pistols. Normal .45 bullets are most common.

Silver Bullets - Effective against Werewolves.

Mercury bullets - Special bullets for killing demons.

Aqua Vampira Bullets - Special bullets that are highly lethal against Vampires.

Shells - Ammunition for the shotgun.

Fuel - Gas for use in the flamethrower.

NOCTURNE

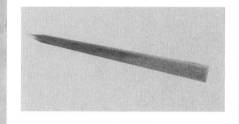

Crossbow bolts - Wooden bolts used for crossbow ammunition.

Blessed Crossbow Bolts - Wooden stakes carved with holy symbols. Very useful for killing powerful undead, such as Ghouls.

Tommy Gun Drum - Ammunition for a Tommygun.

NOCTURNE

CHAPTER FOUR: GEAR

Elephant Gun shells - Massive shells for a massive gun.

Inventory

In addition to his weapons, the Stranger can carry various items in his overcoat pockets. These are accessed by cycling through the inventory (default keys). Once you've selected the item to use, press the ACTION key or button to use it.

Health

The Stranger won't survive long without medical attention. Health can be used from inventory like any other item, or it can be set to be AUTO USED from the OPTIONS menu. There are two types of health restoratives the Stranger can use:

Doctor's bag - Each doctor's bag contains various bandages and other healing items that will restore the Stranger's health when used.

Liquor - A good stiff drink will restore a measure of health, but won't have nearly the effect of more serious medical attention.

THE OFFICIAL STRATEGY GUIDE

Keys

The Stranger will encounter many locked doors in his travels, and the only way to enter them is to use a key of some sort. In most cases, these are simple door keys, but keys can also be artifacts, buttons, levers, or switches. It is very rare that you'll find a locked door that can't be opened in some manner. If you have the key that opens a door in your inventory, the locked door will open when you push the ACTION button near the door.

Lantern (special)

The Stranger can attach a light, or lantern, to his weapons, enabling him to see in even the darkest surroundings. To use it, press the FLASHLIGHT key. Press the key again to turn it off. The lantern is only as strong as its batteries, which will lose power the longer the light is on. Once the lantern battery is completely drained, it will have to be recharged before it can be used again.

You will find batteries in various areas that can greatly extend the length of the light's usefulness. However, they will eventually need to be recharged to be of any use.

NOCTURNE

NOCTURNE
Official Strategy Guide

Dark Reign of the
Vampire King

Chapter Five – Act One

THE OFFICIAL STRATEGY GUIDE

Act 1: Germany, 1927

Something's not right in the area near Gaustadt Castle in Germany. Supernatural activity is on the rise in the area, and Spookhouse operatives, the Stranger and Svetlana Lupescu, are being dispatched to discover the cause of the increase in activity, and to bring back a legendary artifact rumored to be in the area.

Act 1, Scene 1: Spookhouse HQ

(The Stranger emerges from the elevator in the basement of the Phillip Howard Federal Building. Colonel Hapscomb meets him, and they walk toward the secret office.)

Colonel: Stranger, thank you for coming in on such short notice.

You will have control of the Stranger once the Colonel has given the password and the secret panel opens.

(They enter the "front" office and face a prim secretary in an almost empty office.)

Colonel: The world is a dark place.

Secretary: Who will protect the world from darkness?

Colonel: We will.

(A panel in the wall opens to reveal the secret entrance. The Stranger and the Colonel stride through. As they walk down the hall to the elevator and further into HQ, they talk.)

NOCTURNE

CHAPTER FIVE: ACT ONE

Continue to follow the Colonel down the hallway to the elevator.

Colonel: I suppose I should tell you: you'll have a partner on this mission.

Stranger: A partner? Who?

Colonel: Svetlana Lupescu. I know you don't really like her, Stranger, but –

Stranger: I don't "like" anyone. I hate monsters.

Colonel: I wouldn't call her a monster. She's only half vampire.

Stranger: Half is too much.

Colonel: But it's that half of her that makes her so ideal for this assignment. You've put aside your personal feelings in the past, Stranger. I trust you'll do the same now.

Stranger: If she crosses me, she dies.

Colonel (with a sigh): I'm sure she feels the same about you.

By this time, they are at the briefing room. Follow the Colonel into the briefing room, where Svetlana will greet you.

NOCTURNE

Svetlana: Nice to see you again, Stranger. I look forward to working with you.

(The Stranger sits. The lights dim. The projector lights, showing appropriate images.)

Colonel: Have either of you ever heard of the Yathfoe-Gyoule stone?

Svetlana: The Yathgy?

Colonel: Then you've heard of it. I suspected you might.

Svetlana greets the Stranger

Svetlana: Only through legend. It's the "Holy Grail" of the vampire world. The vampire who wields it is said to be immune to those things that would kill any other vampire. He can walk anywhere, even in sunlight, and strike down man or beast with a thought.

Colonel: Yes, those are the legends. Some even suggest that the stone is the petrified heart of an ancient vampire. But legends aside, we think we've tracked down the artifact.

Svetlana: I always thought that it was just as much a myth as the Holy Grail.

Stranger (knowingly): What makes you think the Grail is a myth?

Colonel (after a flummoxed pause brought on by the Stranger's enigmatic response): Yes, well, we think we might have found the Yathfoe-Gyuole stone. Our intelligence suggests that a castle in Germany by the name of Gaustadt was the last known location of the artifact. Rumors, of course, but reports of strange creatures and supernatural events have been becoming suspiciously more frequent over the past century. Whether the stone is there or not, something is drawing the supernatural to that mountain.

NOCTURNE

CHAPTER FIVE: ACT ONE

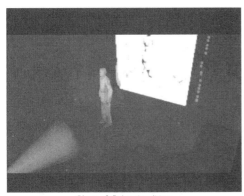
Shot of Colonel talking

Stranger (displeased): This is beginning to sound like a research assignment.

Colonel: It's far more important than that. Your mission is to retrieve the artifact. We've surveyed the region as best we can. Reports that have trickled out over the past hundred years indicate that the journey itself to the castle will be treacherous.

Svetlana: Why is it so important to retrieve this stone? No one here can utilize its full potential.

Svetlana: I suspect that not even I would benefit from its powers since my half-human blood gives me many of the benefits this stone is rumored to bestow.

Colonel: As you know, our trophy hall is filled with weapons and artifacts of great power that would allow an individual to rule the world, should he wield them properly. By keeping them here under lock and key, we can ensure that they never fall into the wrong hands.

Stranger: Why not simply destroy them?

Colonel: Some cannot be destroyed. We've tried. Others may prove... useful to us in the future. In the event of another Great War, we have weapons that would guarantee our victory against any odds. Returning to business, we've done some preliminary reconnaissance. Our operatives couldn't penetrate very deeply into the foothills. The entire area is crawling with werewolves.

Svetlana (jabbing at Stranger playfully): I thought you killed all the werewolves in Germany.

NOCTURNE

Stranger (grunts, annoyed by her jest): Hmm.

Colonel: We tried to find relatives or friends of anyone from the Gaustadt region. We couldn't find one person with any connection to the area. We do know that small villages in the area were inhabited as late as the 1850's, but since then, no one has had any first-hand contact with anyone from that region. All the information you need is on your desks, and your travel arrangements have been made. Good luck, and be careful.

(Svetlana rises and walks out.)

Svetlana: Meet me at the elevator when you're ready to leave, Stranger.

Feel free to wander around the offices for a while. While talking to everyone in the office will gain you some information, no one but Doc Holliday has anything you need for this mission. Talk to Hiram, who is seated just outside the briefing room, then enter the gym (located to Hiram's right). Once you're done talking to Moloch, Khen, and Haystack, leave the gym and head for the lab (located to Hiram's left). Inside, you'll find Doc Holliday.

(Doc Holliday is dissecting a body or doing something scientific.)

Holliday: Stranger, can you come back later? As you can see, I'm extremely busy.

(Returns to work.)

Stranger: I have to leave on a mission soon.

Holliday: I see. And you want to know if I have any goodies for you. What's the mission?

Stranger: Werewolves and vampires.

Stranger with Holliday

Holliday: Vampires? Svetlana just returned from her last mission; I don't suppose she's going on this mission with you, is she?

NOCTURNE

CHAPTER FIVE: ACT ONE

Stranger: Yes.

Holliday (amused at the pairing): Interesting. Well, I've got the standard aqua vampira that Hamilton Killian helped develop. "Better than holy water," he always said. And I have a new item that I just finished. I haven't had time to field-test it yet. Basically, it produces artificial sunlight. It takes a while to charge up, but when it does, it ought to fry any vampire and, at the very least, temporarily blind anything else.

Holliday: You'd better not accidentally shoot a team member with it. Especially Svetlana. (to herself) Hmm... I wonder if this machine will even have an effect on a dhampir? (back to regular conversation). Either way, it might not be a good idea to use this if you and Svetlana are going to be in close proximity during the mission.

Stranger testing Sun of God

Stranger (not to be denied): I'll take my chances. What do you call it?

Holliday: It's the Charged Radiance Emitter, or, more colorfully, "The Sun of God."

Stranger: Nice. Anything else?

Holliday: Werewolves, huh? Where did you say you're going?

Stranger (hesitant, expecting the same jibes as from Svetlana): Germany.

Holliday (attempting the same joke Svetlana used earlier): I thought you killed all—

Stranger (quickly interrupting, annoyed): What else do you have?

Holliday: Sorry, Stranger, just the standard silver bullets. I've been very busy. You're lucky I was able to finish "The Sun" before your mission.

NOCTURNE

(Holliday returns to work.)

Walk to Holliday's workbench and collect the Doctor's Bag and all the Silver Bullets on it. If the Stranger tries to get anything else from the counter, Holliday will scold him. Once you have everything you can get, leave the lab and meet Svetlana at the elevator. Open the elevator door to start the mission.

Act1, Scene 2 – Village Falkenburg

(Outside the city wall, the Stranger and Svetlana emerge from the tangled mess of mountain trails that have isolated the village for centuries. As they pass a small cemetery, the fresh earth of one of the graves begins to shift, and a body rises from the muck. The Stranger draws his weapons.)

Stranger: Watch out!

Svetlana: Wait! This one's not a monster.

Stranger: Are you crazy? He just climbed out of a grave.

Svetlana: I'm telling you, he smells of life.

(By this time, the man, Tormah Klienshenck, has risen fully and dusted himself. He starts running when he sees the heroes. The Stranger steps before him to stop him.)

Stranger: Who are you?

Tormah (half mad, frantic and panicking): Sentinels! No! They're everywhere!

Svetlana: Sentinels? Who are these sentinels?

Tormah: Huge, monstrous things! Hideous things that will devour you whole!

Stranger: Come on, Svetlana. He's crazy.

Tormah (laughs hysterically): Ha, ha, ha! I'm crazy? You've come here of your own free will? You're crazy! You'll never escape.

NOCTURNE

CHAPTER FIVE: ACT ONE

Stranger: You obviously escaped.

Tormah: Yes. But I'm not crazy. I'm a genius! I hid in a coffin with my friend's corpse, so when they buried him out here, I could escape!

(The sound of leathery wings in the distance frightens Tormah. He flees.)

Tormah (as he flees): They've found me!

(Once Tormah is gone...)

Stranger: What was that all about?

Svetlana: I'm not sure. He was totally mad. But one thing I am sure of: there are vampires here. I can smell them. Did you see the bite marks on his neck?

Stranger: Yes.

The gates of the town below are locked, so you need to find a way in. Don't go down the hill just yet. Head for the small crypt on the same hill as the grave from which Tormah crawled. A gated opening in a small crypt will grab the Stranger's attention.

Stranger: I can feel air coming from this crypt. It smells like fresh air. It might open into the town somewhere.

The gate on the crypt is locked, so you need to find a key that will open it. Head down the hill and walk around the right side of the town walls. About midway down the wall, you'll see a pair of dead bodies and a box on the ground. Get the key on the ground near the first body, but watch out; the other Ghoul isn't dead. Kill it, then search the box to find 200 Bullets. Return to the crypt at the top of the hill and use the key to open the gate.

NOCTURNE

CHAPTER FIVE: ACT ONE

Stranger: Let's go.

(After a few steps in, Svetlana stops.)

Svetlana (grabbing her head in pain): I can't go on! We're nearing holy ground.

Stranger: We just tromped through an entire graveyard, why stop now?

Svetlana (in pain):   That little graveyard was never consecrated. It's not holy. But the ground here burns my skin. To go any further would be suicide.

Stranger (not disappointed at all): Fine. I'll go on alone.

Svetlana: I'll find another way in.

Stranger: Um-hmm (unspoken "whatever")

(Svetlana turns and moves back towards the graveyard.)

Svetlana: Go ahead and enter the village through the crypt. Try to open the front gate. In the meantime, I'll look for another way in.

THE OFFICIAL STRATEGY GUIDE

Enter the open crypt. The Stranger emerges in a decrepit, long-abandoned church. Outside, the town is deserted. As the Stranger enters the street, a Sentinel will swoop down from above. Using regular bullets, aim up at its head, and back up to give yourself room to avoid its attacks, then blast it until it's dead.

Open the gate at the end of the street by pushing the lever on the wall beside it. You must kill the Sentinel to be able to open the gate and allow Svetlana to enter from outside. Otherwise, you must fight the other Sentinels on your own.

(Once the gate is opened):

Svetlana: Excellent work. (Looks at Sentinel.) What in the world is this thing? I've never seen anything like it. Whoever summoned this beast must be very powerful.

Stranger: There might be others like it.

Svetlana: Did you find any villagers?

Stranger: Not one. They're either dead or hiding.

Svetlana: With monsters like this roaming the streets, I can't blame them.

NOCTURNE

CHAPTER FIVE: ACT ONE

If you didn't open the gate for some reason, the Stranger will have to kill four Sentinels alone (no easy task). After the fourth Sentinel is killed, Svetlana enters through an unseen chink in the wall and emerges from behind a seemingly inaccessible corner. Together, they hunt down the remaining Sentinels.

While you search for Sentinels, enter the pub and get the Doctor Bag behind the bar. All other doors in town are locked, and you won't be able to open them. Once all the Sentinels are dead, the village Mayor, Valstav, emerges from hiding.

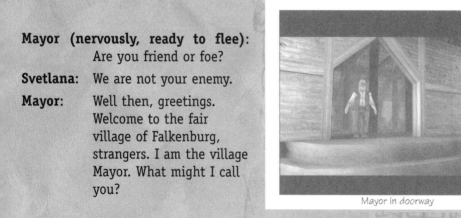
Mayor in doorway

Mayor (nervously, ready to flee): Are you friend or foe?

Svetlana: We are not your enemy.

Mayor: Well then, greetings. Welcome to the fair village of Falkenburg, strangers. I am the village Mayor. What might I call you?

THE OFFICIAL STRATEGY GUIDE

Svetlana: I am Svetlana Lupescu.

Stranger: "Stranger" is fine.

Mayor: Very well. I have no idea how you found our little village; it matters not, I suppose. You should return now the way you came. You are both in terrible danger.

Svetlana: What? You mean these creatures? We can handle ourselves.

Mayor (worried about the dead creatures and what it portends): But don't you see? It is only a matter of time before an army of those things is sent to replace those you have slain. Please leave. It will benefit no one for two more people to suffer as our town suffers.

Stranger: We didn't come this far to be dissuaded by one man's opinion. Tell us what you know, and keep it brief. You can worry about our safety later.

talking to Mayor

Mayor: A great evil has befallen us. You've seen some signs of that evil here. The oppression from Castle Gaustadt has become more and more severe since we settled in this valley after the bloody reign of Andronicus Comnenus.

Svetlana: Andronicus? Andronicus ruled in the twelfth century.

Mayor: Impressive. You know our history well. Our people have been here a long time, and each year our village falls deeper into ruin. I fear we've only a few years left. And because of your actions today, we might have even less time. Count Voicu's wrath will descend upon this innocent town when he learns his Sentinels have been slain.

NOCTURNE

CHAPTER FIVE: ACT ONE

Stranger: Count Voicu?

Mayor: He is the master of Castle Gaustadt, beyond the forest on the mountain that overlooks this valley.

Svetlana: Tell us about this Count. He's not a normal man, is he?

Mayor: What do you mean?

Svetlana: He's a vampire, is he not?

Mayor (shocked): Well, yes. That is rumored to be so. Why would you suspect such a thing?

Svetlana: I can smell it. And there were bite marks on a man outside this village.

Mayor: Man? What man?

Svetlana: He didn't tell us his name. He was babbling, warning us about the sentinels.

Mayor: Did he say anything else?

Stranger: That's all.

Mayor: How did he escape? The sentinels don't let us wander from town.

Svetlana: Apparently he hid in a coffin with a corpse and was buried outside of town.

Mayor: How clever. Well, at least one person has escaped the Count's iron grip. If that madman truly is a vampire, think of the horrors he must be inflicting upon our children!

Svetlana: Your children?

Mayor: Over the past year, the Count has taken all of our daughters, for what vile purpose we can only guess. We tried to fight back, but his Sentinels are too many and too strong.

Svetlana: Now that the Sentinels are gone, we recommend that you flee the city.

Mayor: Never! This is our home. We may die defending it, but we will not run like cowards! We are a proud people, and if we leave, our daughters will surely die.

NOCTURNE

THE OFFICIAL STRATEGY GUIDE

(The Mayor studies the Stranger and Svetlana briefly before offering:)

Mayor: I will not ask you to involve yourselves in this horror, but it's obvious that you are capable warriors. If you offer your help, we will accept it. But we will not leave this town.

Svetlana: We'll discuss the matter with this Count Voicu. If we can't reason with him…

Stranger (interrupting, forcefully): We will kill him.

Mayor: Our humble village appreciates your help. I pray—for the sake of our town and our children—that you are successful.

Once you've finished with the Mayor, talk to the villager in the room with him. The Stranger's abrupt and intimidating manner won't go over well, so Svetlana will have to take over talking to him (you still use the Stranger to start the conversation, but Svetlana will do the talking). One of the townsmen will mention Yuri, a trapper who lives deep in the woods. There are liberated villagers in various areas, so seek them out to find out what they have to say. However, the longer you stay in town, the more Ghouls will come looking for you, so don't hang around long.

NOCTURNE

CHAPTER FIVE: ACT ONE

Once you're through talking to towns-people, open the gate near the Town Hall and exit through it to enter the forest.

Act1, Scene 3 – The Forest

Just outside the town walls, the Stranger and Svetlana enter the forest as rain begins to fall. Follow the path under the fallen tree ahead and approach the wrecked wagon. Search the area near the wagon to find a Doctor's Bag.

Svetlana: The smell of werewolves is overwhelming. They are all around us.

Stranger: Why don't they attack?

Svetlana: They're toying with us. Surrounding us. They will attack soon enough. Look at this horse. Flesh torn from shattered bones.

Continue along the path until you reach a fork in the path. Visible down the right-hand path are two bodies.

Svetlana (surprised): It's a vampire!

Stranger: Staked through the heart. Is it holding another stake? Why would a vampire carry a stake?

Svetlana: A civil war among the vampires?

Stranger: There's a werewolf carcass over here. Must've been quite a fight.

Get the stake from the ground in front of the dead vampire, and continue down the left path (the right-hand one dead ends). You'll reach another fork; veer left and approach the small hut ahead. If you talked to the townsman who told you about Yuri, Svetlana will call out to him.

Svetlana (shouting from outside the shack): Yuri! We've come from Village Falkenburg. We're traveling to Castle Gaustadt.

CHAPTER FIVE: ACT ONE

Stranger: I don't think anyone's home.

Svetlana: The smell of life is fresh here. Someone was here recently, but he is gone now.

There is nothing of interest in or around the shack. Just to the right of the shack, you can make out a faint path that leads behind the shack. Follow it deeper into the forest, and you'll come to a wooden bridge that spans a dam ahead. Cross over the bridge to reach the causeway on the other side, where you'll see a mill on your left. Walk down the stone steps on your left, then walk up the wooden stairs to the mill. Follow the balcony to the front of the mill, where Svetlana will speak up again.

Svetlana (shouting from outside the mill): Yuri! We've come from Village Falkenburg. We're traveling to Castle Gaustadt.

Yuri: Please come in. These woods are dangerous. Traveling to Castle Gaustadt? You choose a poor place to visit. Count Voicu does not welcome guests.

Svetlana: We've come to stop Count Voicu.

NOCTURNE

THE OFFICIAL STRATEGY GUIDE

Stranger: Kill him, if necessary.

Yuri: Then my prayers are with you. My mastery is over the forest. If I thought I stood a chance of beating him, I would have traveled to the castle years ago and killed the Count myself. I'm safe from him here. He avoids the forest and the werewolves that live here.

Yuri: In an ironic way, I owe those beasts my life. My people once were gypsies, well versed in the darker arts. One of our talents was the art of skinwalking. When we first fell under Voicu's thumb, a troop of our bravest men volunteered to wear the skin of the wolf and take to the forests to protect us from the Count. Eventually, he learned to make the winged ones that can pass over the forest instead of through it. The manwolves grew restless, hungry.

Yuri: After centuries of walking as beasts, our protectors forsook their allegiance to us and grew feral. Our once-warriors began to stalk us. They became as great a threat to us as Voicu himself. Now, only I survive. Those of my people not devoured by the wolves were taken by the vampires.

Yuri: Take whatever traps and medicines you think you can use. The traps can be used repeatedly. They are not lethal, but they can slow down the fiercest of beasts. Beware the traps I've hidden throughout these woods. Some are very lethal, and they do not discriminate between man and beast.

Yuri will lead the Stranger and Svetlana upstairs. Along the wall, you'll find a Doctor's Bag, some Silver Bullets in a small chest, two wolf traps, a Woodsman's Axe, a Crossbow with 20 wooden bolts, and 70 Blessed Crossbow Bolts. Collect everything; you're done here, so return to the shack across the dam and follow the other fork in the path. Beware—Yuri has set some nasty traps in the woods ahead.

NOCTURNE

CHAPTER FIVE: ACT ONE

The first trap is nearby. You'll see a pile of Werewolf bodies ahead. Slow down and proceed carefully. The trap is triggered by a barely visible rope that crosses the path. When the swinging log is triggered, stand still and wait for it to stop, then walk around it.

You'll see a dead Vampire and a dead Werewolf ahead; follow the path near the road marker. This will take you past another dead Werewolf. Make sure you have Silver Bullets loaded and your pistols drawn before continuing.

Follow the path past the dead Werewolf. An ambush of three Werewolves is waiting ahead. As soon as the camera angle switches, open fire on them as they leap from the trees around you. The Stranger's Silver Bullets will make quick work of them, allowing you to continue.

Four more Werewolves will ambush you just ahead. Take them down with Silver Bullets again. Keep following the path through the tunnel ahead. Approach the large clearing past the next road marker with caution; there are several Werewolf ambushes around it. Make good use of Yuri's wolf traps at the first sign of an ambush; they will hold off two Werewolves while you take care of the others.

If you walk left of the road marker before entering the clearing, you'll be ambushed by four Werewolves. As you walk, watch out for the pits Yuri has dug to trap Werewolves. You can barely see them; stay to the sides of the path to avoid them.

NOCTURNE

CHAPTER FIVE: ACT ONE

Near the back of the clearing, you'll find a narrow path through the trees. Follow it and kill the Werewolves—there are two ambushes of four Werewolves each back here—and follow the path deeper into the forest.

Past the next road marker, you'll come to a wooden suspension bridge.

Svetlana: This bridge doesn't look too safe. I think we should try to find another way across.

Walk to the left along the cliff edge. When you come to the end of the cliff, Svetlana will make a super-human jump across the chasm. The Stranger must return to the bridge and cross. On the way back, two more Werewolves will ambush you, so be prepared and kill them.

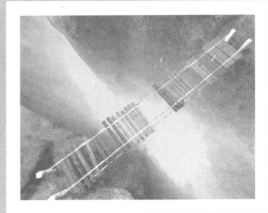

> TIP: You can avoid the harrowing crossing by stepping outside the guide ropes and walking across on the support cables.

Svetlana will reappear once the Stranger is across, and you can proceed to the castle ahead.

NOCTURNE

CHAPTER FIVE: ACT ONE

Act 1, Scene 4 – Castle Gaustadt

As you approach the castle, the Stranger and Svetlana decide to split up to search for the Count.

As the Stranger enters the castle, you'll see the closed gates ahead. Duck into the small doorway on your left to enter the courtyard beyond. Kill the Ghoul that comes from the small crypt, then enter the doorway ahead.

Turn right and walk past the dead Vampire Bride. A Sentinel will attack from overhead—kill it and keep going. Just past the dead Vampire ahead, two Gargoyles will come to life and attack. Shatter them quickly, then kill the Sentinel that attacks.

In the outer courtyard of the castle, you'll find the chapel. Enter and push the statue of the monk onto the symbol in the center of the room. This will slide back a panel in the floor that reveals a Holy Artifact. Get it, and return to the area just outside the castle doors.

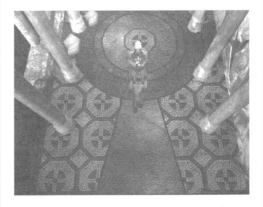

NOCTURNE

CHAPTER FIVE: ACT ONE

When all is clear, open the doors to the castle and kill the four Ghouls inside. There are three doors here. You can reach the throne room directly ahead through any door. Inside the throne room, kill the Gargoyles and Ghouls that attack. Behind the dais is a small chamber with several Ghouls inside. Lure them into the throne room and destroy them.

Climb the stairs in this chamber and get the Bullets and Wooden Stakes from the chests above, as well as the Restorative Tonic from the table. Return to the throne room and walk all the way across it to enter the room opposite the thrones.

Walk up the stairs and kill the two Bats above. Open the cell door in this room and get the Restorative Tonic and Bullets from the chests inside. Follow the stairs up; these stairs will take you to the castle roof. Once on the roof, kill the Bat guardians. Go toward the two towers and enter the one on the right. Kill the Ghoul above and get the tower key on the roof. This key opens the door in the other tower. Cross over to it and open the door.

Kill the Vampire inside with Wooden Crossbow Bolts and get the Bell Tower Key from the chest above. Jump through the hole in the wall to the stairs below and climb up to the top. Climb the next set of stairs, where you'll meet Svetlana again.

NOCTURNE

CHAPTER FIVE: ACT ONE

Stranger: Svetlana! Do you need any help?

Svetlana: I don't need help. You're the one who needs help.

She takes one swipe at the Stranger and flees before he pulls his guns.

Stranger (mutter to himself): What the hell? Crazy bitch!

Servant (from behind the Stranger, entering room): She's not the woman you knew before.

Stranger: Who the hell are you?

Servant: To serve my master, I need no name.

Stranger: What do you know about her?

Servant: The dhampir? She's been changed like all the others.

Stranger: How did you know she was half-vampire?

Servant: The Count has taken particular interest in her ever since the two of you arrived. Her special abilities will be of great use to him.

Stranger: There's no way she would ever serve a man like the Count.

Servant: Believe me. She is not the woman you brought here. When the Count takes a woman as his bride, she changes. She belongs to him now.

Stranger: Bullshit. She leaves with me.

THE OFFICIAL STRATEGY GUIDE

Servant: As long as the Count lives, none of his brides will leave. With you or anyone else.

Stranger (cocking guns): Very well, then.

Servant: Don't be a fool. You can't kill him. He's immortal.

Stranger: If you only knew how many immortal creatures I've killed...

(A loud noise startles the boy, sending him running away.)

Servant: Someone comes!

A Sentinel drops from above. Blast it, then open the bell tower door and enter. Inside, there are several Vampires hanging upside down from the rafters. They won't move to attack unless disturbed. You can open the chest safely without awakening them. Watch out for the hole in the floor; a fall through it is certain death.

NOCTURNE

CHAPTER FIVE: ACT ONE

Inside the chest is a Special Book. Get it, and go back down to the roof near the two towers.

Kill the Bats on the way, and enter the room on the other side of the roof. The first two rooms in this narrow hallway have statues inside; blast them. The next room is a trap. As soon as the Stranger enters, three Ghouls attack. Once they are dead, you can find some Restorative Tonic in a chest near the back of this room. Push the lever in the corner to get out of the room.

Continue down the hallway. There are two Vampire Brides through the doorway at the end of this hall. Use Wooden Stakes to the heart to kill them quickly. Follow the main hallway around to the right, and step through the opening into the hallway beyond. Turn right and you'll come to a small courtyard where a Vampire will attack. Kill it, and enter the door across the courtyard.

Follow this hall down the stairs and open the door in the chamber below to enter a dining hall. Enter the doorway at the head of the table and kill the Vampire Bride and Succubus beyond. There are 100 Blessed Crossbow Bolts in a chest inside the first room on your right.

CHAPTER FIVE: ACT ONE

Follow the hall and the Stranger will enter a chamber with a large mirror inside. Open the door across the chamber and kill the Bats that attack. Walk out onto the roof and drop down to the roof below.

Balance your way up the leaning board and jump across the broken platforms to reach the other side. Walk along the top of the wall, and drop through the hole to enter the Library. Do NOT drop onto the ledge outside the Library door; it will break away, dropping the Stranger to his death.

NOCTURNE

Get the key from the shelf inside, and place the Special Book you found in the bell tower on the book stand in the center of the room. This opens a secret panel behind the picture in the Library.

Enter the room behind the painting and kill the Ghoul that attacks from behind you. Get the Dungeon key from the table inside, and walk behind the tapestry nearest the chair to find a Doctor's Bag and some Blessed Crossbow Bolts and Bullets in the chests nearby.

CHAPTER FIVE: ACT ONE

Cross the room and walk up the stairs behind the other tapestry. Push the lever on the landing above to open a secret door in the wall. There are several Vampires waiting for you on the other side; lure them out one at a time and finish them off. This is the room just above the dining hall.

Go back downstairs to the throne room and enter the room opposite the thrones. There is a large, square hole in the floor with a ladder leading down. Climb down and walk through the opening. Follow the stone steps to the bottom and get the Blessed Crossbow Bolts from the chest below. Walk back up and use your Dungeon Key on the barred entrance ahead to enter the dungeon.

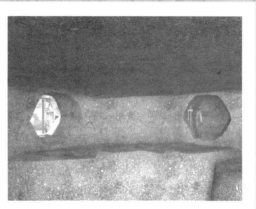

NOCTURNE

Act 1, Scene 5 — Castle Gaustadt Dungeon

The Stranger enters the dungeon in a small room with a skeleton and a chest inside. Open the chest to find 275 Ordinary Bullets, then enter the tunnel ahead. Push the lever to open the gate and drop through the opening.

A Sentinel will attack from above. Finish it off, then push the lever across the room to open the gate ahead. Continue by entering the next room and following the path to the doors across the watery room.

Open the left door and kill the Ghouls at the top of the stairs inside. There's an Imp on the steps inside the next room; kill it and stop on the landing below. Several Vampire Brides (hundreds of years old and looking their age) wait in the room beyond the landing. Kill them and get the Dungeon Key from the table, the Ordinary Bullets and Blessed Crossbow Bolts from the chests in the corner, and the Restorative Tonic from the floor near the ax.

NOCTURNE

Return to the landing in the watery room and open the other door. Walk upstairs and walk behind the open gate. The floor will lower, giving you access to a Dungeon Key. Take it from the alcove and jump below. Cross to the other side and the floor will lower again. Ride it back up and step off.

Kill the Ghouls below and walk down the stairs behind the next doorway. Enter the tunnel below and wait for the Ghoul lurking ahead to come to you. Kill it, then lure the Vampires ahead into the narrow tunnel to finish them off.

Push the two levers in the next room. One opens the bars, and the other raises three platforms in the watery room. Walk through the opening and across the three new platforms to reach the door on the landing ahead.

There is a Ghoul on the stairs ahead; kill it and walk upstairs. Avoid the pendulum in the next room by stepping into the room and side-stepping so you can see the Ghoul beyond it. Kill the Ghoul, then time a run past the swinging pendulum.

NOCTURNE

CHAPTER FIVE: ACT ONE

Now you must complete three perfect jumps to cross the next room. Walk to the edge of each platform, and perform a standing jump. Make sure you are at the edge before jumping, and you'll make it.

Kill the three Vampire Brides in the chamber beyond with Wooden Stakes, then get the Precious Gem from one of the coffins. Repeat the jumps to get back across the pendulum room, then pass the first pendulum.

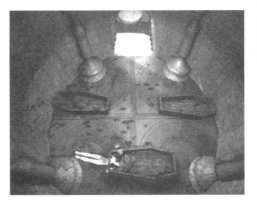

On the lower level of this pendulum room are two doors. Open the only door you can open at this point, and enter the long, narrow hallway. Kill the Ghoul ahead and enter the chamber below.

Place the Precious Gem on the empty pedestal to open a secret door. Get the bullets from the chest behind you, then enter the secret door. Cross into Count Voicu's chamber.

NOCTURNE

CHAPTER FIVE: ACT ONE

Voicu is resting in the coffin in the center of the lava pool. Walk around the room until you can cross the bridge. Voicu will arise and transform into a massive, flying, bat creature. The only weapon that does serious damage to Voicu is the Holy Relic you found in the chapel outside the castle.

Hold a position in the circle, and Voicu will fly to you. Hit him with the Holy Relic as he flies by. Once he has lost 3/4 of his health, he'll transform back to his Vampire form. Stay inside the circle; Voicu calls down stalactites to fall on you, but they will miss if you're in the circle.

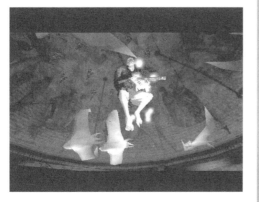

Rush Voicu with the Holy Relic, and finish him off. In his weakened state, he won't be able to resist. There is a Sanctum Key near Voicu's coffin. Take it and return to the pendulum room.

The key opens the other door here; once inside, the Stranger will have to fight the rest of Count Voicu's brides. Stay on the move, and don't waste your fire on the ones that are flying around. When they land, nail them.

NOCTURNE

CHAPTER FIVE: ACT ONE

Once all the brides are destroyed, approach the tapestry in the back of the room, where you'll see some feet sticking out from beneath it.

(The Stranger rips the tapestry from the wall and brings his guns to bear.)

Bride (terrified and crying): Please let me go! I'll do anything, just let me live!

Stranger (demanding harshly): Did you taste the Count's blood?

Bride: I don't know.

Stranger (hostile): Did you taste his blood?

Bride: I don't know what you mean!

Stranger (lowering guns): Very well. I won't hurt you. I'll take you back to Falkenburg.

NOCTURNE

Bride: Falkenburg?

Stranger: Yes, your home—

(The Stranger falls silent and studies the portrait that had previously been hidden by the tapestry.)

Bride: I'm not from Falkenburg.

Stranger (to himself): The Mayor?

Stranger: What do you know of the man in this portrait?

Bride: I've never seen him before.

(Svetlana enters quickly near the Stranger. He levels his gun at her heart.)

Svetlana: Stranger! What are you doing?

Stranger: I'm about to kill you.

Svetlana: Are you out of your mind? How many times do I have to tell you that being half vampire doesn't make me evil?

Stranger: You sound like you're back to normal now.

Svetlana: Almost. I feel like I've been kicked in the head. My ears are ringing. I had to fight off the Count's influence, and it wasn't easy.

Svetlana: I vaguely remember talking to him, but it's all a blur. He drove his own will into my mind and controlled me like a puppet.

Svetlana: I've never had my mind taken over like that before. He was extremely powerful.

Stranger: Not powerful enough.

Svetlana: It's ironic that you saved me, considering our past.

Stranger: We have no past.

NOCTURNE

CHAPTER FIVE: ACT ONE

Svetlana: Try as you might, you can't forget everything.

Stranger: I can.

Svetlana: If you say so. Shall we be off? It looks like we've managed to save at least one of the village's daughters.

Svetlana (to Bride): What's your name?

Bride: Nadia.

Svetlana: Come with us. Your parents in Falkenburg will be delighted to see you.

Stranger: I'm not so sure about that. She's not from Falkenburg. In fact, I don't think anything the mayor told us was the truth. Look at this portrait.

Svetlana: The mayor of Falkenburg?

Stranger: I think he has held other titles in the past.

Svetlana: I knew it! I thought the scent of vampires was too strong in that town. I assumed that the Count and his minions had left that smell. It makes perfect sense, now.

Stranger: What makes perfect sense?

Svetlana: The mayor is the true lord of this castle. The Count was his son. The old vampire and his retainers must have been banished to Falkenburg. Exiled from his own kingdom and herded with werewolves.

Svetlana: The crazy man we met outside the village wasn't escaping from just the Sentinels. He was escaping from the townsfolk themselves. They are vampires, and he was meant to be their food!

Stranger: An entire town of vampires held captive by the Count? Why didn't he just kill them all?

Svetlana: I don't know.

(The Mayor materializes out of nowhere.)

THE OFFICIAL STRATEGY GUIDE

Mayor: Perhaps I can explain.

(The Stranger turns his guns on the mayor.)

Stranger: You made a huge mistake showing yourself now that I know who you are.

Mayor (ignoring the Stranger with an annoyed, amused sigh, addresses Svetlana): Clever girl, this one. I thought she might have been a dhampir when she first came into the village. I thought for sure she would detect us, but she never put the clues together.

Svetlana: So I was right? The Count was your son.

Mayor: Yes. That insolent bastard. Now that you've killed him, my people and I can return home to this castle.

Svetlana: Stranger, put your guns away.

Stranger: You know I have no sense of humor.

(Svetlana steps between the Mayor and the Stranger.)

Svetlana: I'm not joking, Stranger.

Mayor: You'd be wise to do as your friend says.

Stranger: I have no friends.

Mayor: Then you would be wise to make her one.

Mayor: The reason my son did not kill me was because he did not know how to properly utilize the Yathgy. Until I revealed its secret to him, he knew he could not kill me. But I would not give up that secret easily.

Stranger: The Yathgy?

Mayor: Yes. Now that it's back in my control, things can return to normal around here.

Mayor: My son managed to separate me from the Yathgy long enough to overpower me. I've spent the past hundred years waiting for the misused power of this stone to destroy him. Thank you for accelerating the process.

NOCTURNE

CHAPTER FIVE: ACT ONE

Mayor: My followers and I have tried to reclaim the castle by force on a number of occasions. You might have seen the aftermath of those attempts littering the forest and this castle. And beyond my son's resistance, the werewolves of the forest interfered with our attempts as well. There were times when three separate forces met in those accursed woods.

Mayor (to the Stranger): You've proven yourself quite capable. If you weren't a mere human, I'd ask you to join me. As it is, I would be honored if this lady were to join my ranks.

Svetlana: No thanks. I have other obligations.

Mayor: A foolish choice, my dear. Now I suppose there's nothing left for me to do but kill you.

(The Stranger brings his guns to bear again, but the mayor only laughs.)

Mayor (laughing delightedly): But since you've helped me regain my castle and the Yathgy, I'll overlook the fact that you have killed my minions and the brides I have taken the past millennia to collect. You may live. You are free to leave this castle. Take with you this pitiful girl-child who my son failed to make his own bride. But know that if you ever set foot in this house again, you will belong to me.

Svetlana (bowing graciously despite her urge to attack): Thank you, kind sir.

(Svetlana leads the Stranger away.)

Stranger: What about the stone?

Svetlana (quietly to Stranger): The stone stays, Stranger. We leave. Now.

Stranger (tenaciously): Not until our mission is complete.

NOCTURNE

THE OFFICIAL STRATEGY GUIDE

Svetlana: Stranger, you cannot see the things that I see. You must simply trust me when I say that his offer to leave must be taken. His son, the Count, was a frail degenerate compared to him.

Stranger (disgusted): So our mission is a failure?

Svetlana: Not necessarily. I doubt this man will make the same mistake twice. He will not allow another to overthrow him.

Svetlana: And whether the Yathgy is locked in Spookhouse's basement or in this vampire's castle, we at least know where it resides.

Stranger: But he is a bloodsucking vampire! As soon as we leave, he'll be out looking for more food and new brides. Innocent humans will have their lives torn apart.

Svetlana: We'll deal with him when the time is right, but there's nothing the two of us can do about it now, alone. Throwing ourselves at him would be suicide, so calm down..

Svetlana (after a pause, playfully): Besides, you already got to kill a really powerful vampire today, so cheer up.

Stranger (grunts—maybe approvingly, maybe not—at her humor): Hmm.

(Svetlana strides away with the Stranger and Nadia walking slightly grumpily behind her. As they leave, the people from the village arrive at the castle to reclaim their old home.)

NOCTURNE

NOCTURNE
Official Strategy Guide

Tomb of the
Underground God

Chapter Six - Act Two

Act 2 - Texas - 1931

It is four years after the Stranger's somewhat successful mission at Castle Gaustadt in Germany. Strange reports from the small town of Redeye, Texas, have lead Spookhouse to deploy Scat Dazzle, Hiram Mottra, and the Stranger to check out rumors of zombies and monsters terrorizing the town.

Act 2, Scene 1 – The Train

(The Stranger boards the train. In the third class passenger car, he locates his partner, Spookhouse operative Hiram Mottra, with whom he's worked on a few limited occasions. Hiram seems far more nervous and edgy than usual.)

Stranger: Okay, what's the situation?

Hiram: A sheriff in Redeye, Texas, called in a strange request to the authorities in Chanford. The police in Chanford took it as a request for medical assistance, supposedly due to an outbreak of some unknown skin illness. Chanford sent a couple of doctors expecting to find some kind of minor skin fungus or similar malady.

Hiram: We, on the other hand, suspect that the sheriff's references to "zombies" and "monsters" weren't the hysterical ramblings of a small-town police officer. The Chanford doctors failed to report back after spending a day in the small town, so we're sending in our own "doctors." Scat Dazzle is already in Redeye. He'll meet us at the train station.

NOCTURNE

CHAPTER SIX: ACT TWO

Stranger: Why so nervous?

Hiram: I fear that we may be in grave danger.

Stranger (matter-of-factly): It's our job to be in grave danger.

Hiram: I think someone is following me.

Stranger: Who?

Hiram (gradually becoming more and more frantic): I don't know. That's what frightens me. Normally, I can feel the thoughts of anyone who focuses on me, but so far none of the people on this train have expressed any sort of hostility toward me, even in their thoughts. But I can feel the anger aimed at me. It's been boring into my brain since I left Virginia.

Stranger (curious): You can't tell who it is, where it's coming from?

Hiram: No. I can feel a general pressure all around me. There's no direction, or I could track the culprit down.

(Hiram produces a small note and hands it to the Stranger.)

Hiram: I found this in my luggage.

Stranger (reading): "For the insidious crimes against my people, your people will see ruin." What the hell does that mean?

Hiram: I have no idea. What people could we have ruined?

Stranger: I can't think of any people, as such. But we've wiped out entire civilizations of monsters: vampires, werewolves, changelings. Perhaps a survivor of one of our horucide projects is seeking revenge.

(The train suddenly lurches, accelerating.)

Hiram: Something's wrong! We're going too fast!

(Hiram goes white with fear when he feels the presence of the enemy.)

Hiram (frantically): Oh no! I can feel him! He's close! He's close! The one who's been following me... Oh my God, Stranger, it's...

(A massive hairy claw shatters through the window and drags most of Hiram's body out the window before he can finish.)

Stranger (more angry than startled): What the hell?

NOCTURNE

THE OFFICIAL STRATEGY GUIDE

(The Stranger falls back, drawing his guns, but all is suddenly still. He cautiously approaches the broken window, but there is no sign of Hiram or the creature.)

You have control of the Stranger now. There are two people riding in this car that aren't what they appear to be. As the Stranger approaches them, they will transform into Werewolves. However, you can't shoot them until they change. As they change, blast them. It will take several shots, since you have no silver bullets yet, so keep firing until they are down. The back door of the third class passenger car is locked, so head for the front of the car and jump to the car ahead.

Stranger: Damn. I wasn't expecting werewolves. If Hiram packed as extravagantly as usual, I'll bet I can find more appropriate weapons in his baggage.

NOCTURNE

CHAPTER SIX: ACT TWO

Climb one of the ladders to reach the baggage car roof. Climb down either ladder and approach the stack of crates inside. Hiram's crate is on top of the middle stack. Draw the Stranger's pistols and fire at the crates. DO NOT fire at the small crate sitting on the ground—it's dynamite and will leave a small puddle where the Stranger was standing, if you shoot it. One of the crates will fall open, and you'll see Hiram's gear inside. Grab the Doctor's Bag and Silver Bullets inside, then climb the ladder at the front of the car.

The next car forward is a flatbed car with a small shack on the back. There's nothing of interest in the shack, so jump to the car ahead and then climb to the roof. Don't drop down into this car—it's the meat car, and several werewolves are snacking on beef, and at least one passenger, below. Run forward and leap to the tender ahead. Get the ax from the wall near the steps, then climb onto the coal. The train's controls are wrecked, so don't bother going into the engine's cab. Instead, make the leap from the coal to the top of the engine, then climb down the ladder on the left.

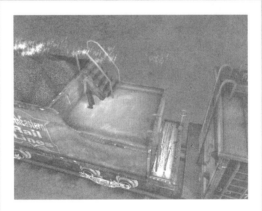

NOCTURNE

The dead engineer here has a key on him. Search him to pocket the key, which the Stranger can use to unlock the rest of the doors on the train. Retrace your steps to the roof of the meat car.

A Werewolf is waiting for you here, so blast it with Hiram's Silver Bullets. When you reach the other end of the car, wait before jumping down. Two Werewolves are waiting below. Aim down at them and pick them off before climbing down. Cross the flatbed car and jump to the baggage car roof.

NOCTURNE

CHAPTER SIX: ACT TWO

Another Werewolf is waiting for you here, so keep your pistols drawn and open fire. Leap to the roof of the third class car, where the Alpha of the Hökkendire tribe will confront the Stranger.

AlphaWerewolf: You! You and all your kind will die! You, who scattered my tribe to the four winds. You thought that you killed us all, but we have survived. You will not survive.

(The Alpha leaps back to the first class car, leaving a handful of minions to slow down the Stranger.)

Stranger: That was the Alpha of the Hökkendire tribe. I had a feeling we didn't wipe them out completely back in '24.

NOCTURNE

Open fire on the two Werewolves the Alpha left behind. Your pistols should target both at once, and the Stranger will have no trouble bringing them down. Climb down the ladder at the rear of the third class car and enter the next one (the key you found on the engineer will unlock the door).

A lady is sitting near the front, but she's no lady. When she turns into a Werewolf, fill her full of hot silver and continue to the back of the car. Kill the other passenger/Werewolf, then open the back door and kill the Werewolf lurking outside.

NOCTURNE

CHAPTER SIX: ACT TWO

Step into the next car, first class, which is completely empty. When the Stranger tries the back door, he'll discover that the door is barred from the other side. Use the ax you found on the tender to break down the door.

Climb to the roof of the first class car, where the Stranger will have the final showdown with the Alpha Werewolf.

AlphaWerewolf: Most formidable. I feel less insulted knowing that it was you who destroyed my tribe. When I've built a new tribe, we will honor your death on this day.

The Alpha is fast, so open fire at once when the cinematic is over, and keep backing up to give the Stranger enough room. Once the Alpha is history, the Stranger will leap from the back of the train.

THE OFFICIAL STRATEGY GUIDE

Act 2, Scene 2 - Redeye, Texas - Population 47

(Fade up to train station. Reverend Jim Maynard greets the Stranger, who is dusting himself off after leaping from the moving train.)

Reverend: Dear Lord! Are you okay, son?

Stranger: I'm fine.

Reverend: I assume you must be Scat Dazzle's partner.

Stranger: Where is he?

Reverend: Eh... I don't know how to tell you this, but he has passed on.

Stranger (skeptical): What happened?

(The Reverend leads the Stranger toward the church.)

Reverend: Please, we can't stay out here. Come with me. I'll explain on the way.

Stranger (referring to the shovel in the Reverend's hand): What's the shovel for?

Reverend: I used to dig graves with it. But it seems all the graves I've dug for the past twenty years weren't deep enough to hold the people I laid to rest.

Stranger: You mean...?

NOCTURNE

CHAPTER SIX: ACT TWO

Reverend: The dead walk.

Stranger (off-handedly): So?

Reverend (flummoxed by Stranger's seeming disinterest): Look, I guess in your line of work, this may not be disturbing, but it's a little bothersome to me. In the past week, I've seen people, who have been dead for a hundred years, rise from their graves. I've seen people I knew when they were alive come back from the dead. But they're not the same. They're monsters!

Stranger: And the shovel?

Reverend: Hmm? Oh, now the only use I have for this thing is as a weapon. It's not in my nature to kill, mind you, but these things are already dead, and they're evil. I'm sure the good Lord doesn't have anything against me knocking their heads off. That seems to be about the only way to put them down for good.

(At this point, they arrive at the church. Scat Dazzle lies inert under debris that apparently fell from the rooftop.)

Reverend: He died guarding the church. He'd holed up on the roof and shot anything that came this way that wasn't human. Something went wrong, and the roof collapsed. He'd said that you were coming to assist him, so I went to meet you when I heard the train coming.

THE OFFICIAL STRATEGY GUIDE

(The Stranger searches through Scat's clothing.)

Reverend: He's dead. I checked.

Stranger: Not for long. Damn. I need rum.

Reverend: I, uh, have some scotch.

Stranger: That won't work; I need rum.

Reverend: There's a saloon in the middle of town. But this really isn't the time.

Stranger: Yes. It is.

The Reverend has some Scotch stashed behind the stained glass directly behind the pulpit. Break the glass and get the Scotch. It won't restore as much health as a Doctor's Bag, but it will help some when the Stranger is injured. When you need to use it, select it from the Stranger's inventory and press ENTER to use it.

Get the shovel that's leaning against the tombstone just outside the church. The shovel can be used as a weapon, but it's a bit different than the weapons the Stranger normally carries. To use it as a weapon, press the DRAW/HOLSTER key. To get rid of it, press the DRAW/HOLSTER key again before putting it down.

NOCTURNE

CHAPTER SIX: ACT TWO

TIP: The biggest problem the Stranger will have on this mission is a lack of ammunition. Don't waste shots on Zombies that aren't attacking. You may not need to shoot them all in order to complete this phase of the mission.

Kill the Zombie that rises from the ground. Head back into town and find the saloon which is just on the left, past the Sheriff's office. There are several zombies around, so use the shovel to put them down.

Kill the zombie and zombie dog that attack in front of the saloon, then enter the saloon and get the bottle of Rum from the counter. If you're using the shovel as a weapon, you'll need to put it down before getting the Rum.

It's not necessary that you do so yet, but if you're feeling adventurous, there are two zombies upstairs that you can easily finish off with the shovel. Once you leave the saloon, hurry back to the church.

Approach Scat's body and use the ACTION key on it, to get the Stranger to revive him.

Stranger (to Reverend): You might want to turn away. I suspect your religious sensibilities might be offended by what I'm about to do.

(Ignoring the reverend, the Stranger sprinkles dust from the pouch he'd found on Scat. Lights and smoke abound. From within a small cloud emerges the form of the Baron. The Stranger offers the cigar and rum.)

NOCTURNE

CHAPTER SIX: ACT TWO

Baron: Ah, the legendary Stranger. The man of mystery. You know, your dark past is not so secret in my realm. I know all about you.

Stranger (flatly): Fascinating. Just revive Scat and be on your way.

Baron (laughing at Stranger's impertinence): Easy, mon. Don't forget who you're dealing with.

Stranger: You have your cigar. You have your rum. All the blood you need is in a pool beneath your host. Do your business and be off.

Baron: Heh! Pray you never owe me a favor.

(The Baron kneels over the form of Scat's wrecked body. More lights and smoke, and Baron Samedi fades away. When the smoke clears, Scat slowly stands, shaking his head.)

Scat: What happened?

Stranger: You died. Again. I used your powder to summon Baron Samedi. He revived you.

Scat: Hey, thanks. There are still people out there. I've heard them crying for help. Find them and bring them here. I still feel a little weak, but I can stay here and guard this place. Once I feel a little stronger, I'll come out and help you.

Stranger: Very well.

Reverend: There are a couple of farmhouses on the other side of town. I haven't had the courage to go there myself, but the Jenkins and the Smiths were alive the last time I saw them.

Stranger: I'll bring them back, and anyone else I find.

It's showtime. The rest of your time in Redeye will be spent rescuing the Smiths, Jenkins, and any other townspeople you find. Unfortunately, the supernatural presence of Baron Samedi has caused the zombies to become very active, so the Stranger will have to battle through them to reach the townfolk.

Scat won't come along, but he can still be useful. Since he has all his gear with him, he has plenty of ammo. The first thing you should do is to clear out the zombies along the main street.

Get them to follow the Stranger, and lead them back to the church, where Scat will take care of them. Once the streets are clear, start looking for people to rescue. You can rescue them in any order, but you can't let any of them die or the mission will end in failure.

NOCTURNE

CHAPTER SIX: ACT TWO

There are a few buildings that don't have townfolk in them, but they do have items that will help the Stranger. The first of these is the Telegraph Office, located near the train depot. There are two zombies inside, and you won't be able to lure them out, so blast them in the head once you're inside. Get the Doctor's Bag in the small office, and leave the building.

The first person you'll find is Buford Elliot. He's cowering in the outhouse across from the Sheriff's office. Open the door to the outhouse, and he'll come out.

Buford:	Oh, dear, sweet mother of mercy! Don't kill me!
Stranger:	I'm here to help. You'll be safe in the church. Finish your business, and I'll take you there.

(Once the Stranger leads him to the church):

Buford:	You're an honest-to-God hero, you know that?

Stranger: Yes.

(Further conversation with Buford isn't productive, but is a bit amusing):

Buford: I've been hiding in that outhouse for two days!

Stranger: I can tell.

THE OFFICIAL STRATEGY GUIDE

Return to the main street and enter the Sheriff's office. Inside, Deputy Dan is locked inside a holding cell.

Deputy Dan: Die!

(He fires his shotgun at the Stranger, but misses, due to his handicapped state.)

Stranger: Settle down, I'm here to help. Shoot at me again and you'll lose the other arm. I'm gathering everyone together in the church for safety.

Deputy Dan (resigned): I'm safe enough right here. That door is locked, and no one's going to get in here.

Stranger: But you're wounded.

Deputy Dan: I'll be fine.

Stranger: You can't even cock that shotgun, much less aim it with only one arm. Come with me, and you'll be safe.

Deputy Dan (after a moment of thought): I guess you're right. But I can't leave this cell. I don't have a key. The sheriff took it with him when he went to check on the saloon.

You can't free the deputy until you find the Sheriff. Before leaving the jail, get the Doctor's Bag and the bullets from the shelf and chest next to it, then leave and head for the saloon.

NOCTURNE

CHAPTER SIX: ACT TWO

The sheriff, now a zombie like most of the other citizens of Redeye, sits at the bar out of long, mindless habit. Kill him and search the corpse for the key to Dan's cell.

Walk upstairs and kill the zombie trying to batter down the door above. Dixie Buttercup, Redeye's only surviving human prostitute, is behind the door.

Daisie: Help! Somebody please help!

Stranger: Let me in. I will take you to the church. You'll be safe there.

Daisie (frantic, from inside the room): How do I know you're not another one of those monsters?

Stranger: Because they don't offer to help.

(After a moment, she opens the door and follows the Stranger.)

THE OFFICIAL STRATEGY GUIDE

Don't open the two doors flanking Dixie's. There are two prostitute-turned-zombies inside you won't have to fight unless you open those doors. Open the door closest to the stairs, and take Dixie down the back stairs. Kill the zombies in the way, head for the church and drop her off, then return to get Dan.

Dan will give you his shotgun. Before leaving the cell, search the chest here to find some shotgun shells.

As you leave the jail, you'll be ambushed by four zombies. Hold a position in the doorway to protect Dan, and blast away. An upward-aimed blast will remove the heads from zombies at close range, so keep blasting away until all is quiet. Dan moves very slowly, but then, so would most people if one of their arms had been chewed off. You'll face some more zombies on the way back to the church. Kill them in the same way and deliver Dan.

You're done rescuing people along the main street. Now it's time to head to the other side of town and find Ma and Pa Smith, who are holed up on the second floor of their farmhouse.

NOCTURNE

CHAPTER SIX: ACT TWO

Once you're across town, take the path to the right and blast the two zombies headed your way. Follow the path to the Smith's farmhouse.

As you near the house, the Smith's zombie dog will attack, and a zombie cow will wander towards the Stranger. Kill them both, then enter the house.

There's nothing on the first floor of the house. Before going upstairs, enter the basement through the doorway across from the front door. Below, you'll find two zombies munching on someone; blow them away, then cross to the door in the corner.

Two zombies will crash through the door. Take them down, then enter the room beyond. You'll find some bullets in the chest here, as well as two boxes of dynamite. Throwing the switch on the wall turns on the outside lights, and also triggers another zombie to crawl from the floor. Be careful where you shoot—if you hit the dynamite, it's all over.

CHAPTER SIX: ACT TWO

You don't need the dynamite, so go back upstairs and head for the second floor. Once on the landing, enter the doorway on the left and blast the zombie that crashes through the window above the desk. Once he's dead, open the chest in the corner to find some shotgun shells.

In the next room, you'll find Ma and Pa Smith.

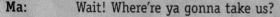

Pa (brandishing pitchfork): Get back, fiend! I'll do ya'in, just like I did all your other demon kin!

Stranger: Calm down, old man. If you want to stay alive, come with me.

Pa: Forget it! We're staying right here till this whole thing passes over.

Stranger (turning to leave): It's your funeral.

Ma: Wait! Where're ya gonna take us?

Stranger: You'll be safe at the church.

Pa: That's all the way across town. How are we supposed to get there?

Stranger: Just follow me.

Ma: Well... okay. We'll follow you.

As soon as the Stranger finishes talking to Ma and Pa, a zombie crashes through the bedroom window. Get in front of the Smiths and blast it before it gets one of them.

Get the Stranger in front of the Smiths, and lead the way downstairs. Kill the zombies inside, then go out onto the porch. Block the doorway so the Smiths can't get by, and blast the zombie that comes crashing through the window on the Stranger's left. There are four more zombies in the yard, so get well in front of the Smiths and take care of them. Run ahead and kill the zombie in the lane ahead, then go back for the Smiths.

As you walk through town, try to outdistance the Smiths and take out any zombies long before they catch up. The Smiths may complain, but it's much easier to do some advance scouting, since the Smiths tend to run right at zombies when they get scared. There are several more zombies in town, so proceed carefully.

Get the Smiths back to church, then go inside and talk to them.

NOCTURNE

CHAPTER SIX: ACT TWO

Ma: Uh, excuse me, sonny, but do you think you could go back and save our children?

Stranger (after aggravated pause): Why didn't you mention that while we were at your house?

Ma: Well, I wasn't sure we could trust you. Now I know that if anyone can save them, you can. They're in the Jenkins' basement, out back of the other farmhouse. They're hiding in the cellar and won't open the door unless they hear our special knock.

(Ma knocks out a well-worn "shave-and-a-haircut" rhythm.)

Stranger (sarcastic): Very original. I'll be right back with your children.

Before you rescue the Smith kids, you need to clear out the Jenkins' farmhouse. On the other side of town, take the other lane that leads to the Jenkins place. Once you reach the farm, walk inside the house and kill the zombies lurking in the sitting room and bedroom.

When you enter the bedroom, you'll see another zombie out the window; shoot it, then grab the bullets and shotgun shells from the dresser.

Go back outside, and start clearing the area of any zombies. There are zombie cows and another zombie near the rundown stable. Kill them, or they will be in the way later. When all is clear, walk around the back side of the house.

NOCTURNE

CHAPTER SIX: ACT TWO

There's another zombie on the roof above the back porch. Draw the Stranger's pistols, and back up until they take aim at the zombie. Fill it full of holes, then kill the zombie struggling to open the cellar door. When the Stranger knocks on the door, the kids will come out. After a quick discussion, they'll follow the Stranger up the stairs.

Although you've killed the zombies in the area, there are more waiting for you. Get in front of the kids and kill the two between you and the path to the Smith's place. As you enter town, you'll be ambushed by several zombies. Don't get cornered, and the shotgun will take care of them in short order.

THE OFFICIAL STRATEGY GUIDE

Once you make it to the church with the kids in tow, the little boy speaks to the Stranger:

Boy: Are you going to hell, now?

Ma: Tommy! Watch your mouth, or you'll get a whippin'!

Boy: But, ma, that's where all the monsters are!

Stranger: Where?

Boy: The pit! I saw lots of monsters in there. It's really the doorway to hell. All the monsters are coming from there. I've seen it.

Pa: He must mean the old mine. It's been abandoned for years and sealed off, but I think the kids have found a way into it.

Stranger (to Scat): What do you think?

Scat: The boy might be right. When I first got here, I noticed it. There's definitely something not right about that place. I asked around, but no one knows much about it.

Reverend: There was an accident there, and the mine was shut down. It's been abandoned for decades.

Reverend: A strange man came into town last winter asking about the old mine. But he disappeared.

Stranger: I'll look into it. How do I get in?

Boy: The gate's locked, but I know how to open it from the inside. I'll help you!

(Cut to mine entrance. Boy climbs through a hidden fissure in the mountain face and disappears briefly. After a tense moment, the gate swings open and the boy runs out.)

NOCTURNE

CHAPTER SIX: ACT TWO

Boy: There you go, mister monster killer!

Stranger: I'll take you back to the church.

Boy (laughing, boasting): Aw, shoot, I can outrun any of those old monsters. I'll go myself.

Stranger: Suit yourself.

(The Boy runs away, and the Stranger enters the mine.)

Act 2, Scene 3 – The Abandoned Mine

(This scene involves no interaction with other characters. The Stranger needs to make his way deep into the mine to discover what is causing the dead in Redeye to terrorize the town.)

The best thing you can do in the mines is run. There are simply too many zombies wandering around for the Stranger to kill them all easily. Unless you get cornered, keep running.

From the mine entrance, follow the tracks until you see the entrances to Tunnel A and Tunnel B. Follow Tunnel B, but make sure you don't fall into the holes along the way. There are at least 10 zombies down this track, but you can get past them easily if you keep going.

You'll reach a fork in the tracks that goes left; stay right and enter Tunnel C. When you come to a long, wooden bridge, slow down and look to your left. Cross the short bridge to the shack on the other side, blasting the zombie inside in the process.

Inside the shack you'll find some shotgun shells, dynamite, a gas mask, and a battery. The battery will make your light last much longer than normal. Grab the goods, then flip on the lights for tunnels A and D, using the switches on the wall.

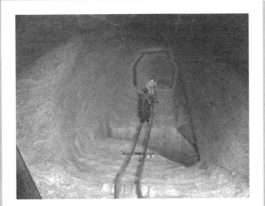

Head back across the wooden bridge and turn right as you exit Tunnel C. This branch of the track goes through Tunnel D. Be careful—there's a huge hole in the floor ahead. You'll have to jump over, so proceed carefully. When you reach the other side, several zombies will attack; use the shotgun to put them out of their misery.

NOCTURNE

CHAPTER SIX: ACT TWO

Follow the tracks in Tunnel D, and you'll pass a ladder on your left. Keep going and kill the two zombies lurking in the storeroom ahead. Be very careful where you shoot—this room is full of dynamite!

Place a crate of dynamite on the transfer platform near the back of the room, and pull the lever to send it up to the transfer room.

Go back up the tracks and climb the ladder. Follow the tracks above until you reach a set of steps and a landing on the Stranger's right. Put the gas mask on, and enter the passage beyond the landing.

NOCTURNE

Inside this chamber, you'll find some shelves with a Doctor's Bag, two bundles of dynamite, and two chests containing shotgun shells and bullets. After you've picked up everything, retrace your steps back up the tunnel to the landing above the ladder the Stranger just climbed.

Make a running jump across to the landing on the other side. You may have to try several times, so it's a good idea to save your game here. To make the jump, you'll need a good running start, and you have to jump at the absolute last second. Falling won't kill you, but it will hurt quite a bit.

Once you've made the jump, follow the tunnel to the transfer room. There are three zombies waiting inside—lure them out and finish them off.

NOCTURNE

CHAPTER SIX: ACT TWO

Pick up the dynamite from the transfer platform on the left and carry it across the room to the other transfer platform. Push the lever to send the dynamite up to the shack in Tunnel C.

Get back to Tunnel C and cross the wooden bridge. The dynamite is across the small bridge near the shack. Cross over and get it, then continue down Tunnel C until you come to a cave-in.

Place the dynamite near the cave-in and back well away. Use the Stranger's pistols to detonate the dynamite, and clear the way for the Stranger to proceed. Put on the Stranger's gas mask—he doesn't really need it now, but when he does, it's better to have it on than to need it and not be able to stop to use it.

NOCTURNE

Head down the tunnel, and you'll encounter some Larvae in a slime pool. They will toss green, glowing chunks of sludge at the Stranger, so just keep moving and you'll be fine. When you come to a dead end, stay left.

Toss dynamite at the group of larvae in the big pool of sludge and, when you've finished them off, enter the small tunnel on the right. You'll have to wade through the slime to get there. Be sure you have your gas mask on—you'll need it now more than ever.

In the next area, RUN! This cavern is filled with larvae, and you have no chance to try and kill them all. Just keep going and stop to kill a larvae only if it's absolutely necessary.

NOCTURNE

CHAPTER SIX: ACT TWO

At the end of the cavern, you'll face your first full-grown Drone. Kill it and enter the narrow doorway ahead.

Act 2, Scene 4 – The Temple of Gardath

The Stranger is nearing his objective. This is the domain of Gardath and his servants, the Drones. The Stranger will have to solve several puzzles in order to finally confront Gardath and try to stop its evil influence on Redeye.

Take the Mystical Stone from its holder. This will unleash two Drones from the ceiling, so back up as you fire to take them down. Pick the pocket of the corpse nearby for some shotgun shells, then continue around the corner.

NOCTURNE

A horde of Drones awaits the Stranger ahead. Many of them will drop in from above, while some will attack from further down the tunnel. Either way, back into a corner to take them all out, then continue along the path.

Eventually, you'll come to a large open area. The massive bulk of Gardath looms overhead on the other side of the chasm, but you aren't ready to cross over and face it yet. Place the Mystic Stone on the pedestal with the red light shooting up from the stone. This will cause the beam to split, and point at each of the four pedestals across the chasm.

Keep following the path, blasting the Drones that attack. Several will ambush you in the long, narrow corridor ahead. Keep your shotgun pointed low and nail them when they appear.

NOCTURNE

CHAPTER SIX: ACT TWO

The platform at the end of the corridor is a lift. Step on and push the lever to raise it. Once you reach the top, follow the passage until you reach a small room with a pedestal on the far side.

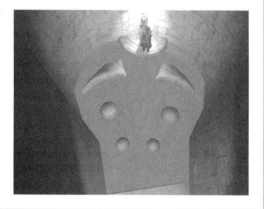

The next Mystical Stone the Stranger needs is here, but this room is a trap. Once you grab the stone, the lighter-colored sand will drain away, leaving only a few platforms for the Stranger to jump across to reach safety. Save your game, then use your pistol sights and your light to aim for the platforms and perform standing jumps until you reach solid ground.

Return to the pedestals beneath Gardath and place the stone on the pedestal that bears the same markings. This will cause the beam to open a door behind Gardath. Enter the door and kill the Drones inside.

The next stone chamber is full of larvae, and the ceiling is studded with metal spears. Cross the room quickly to avoid the larvae and get the stone. As the floor begins to rise, walk into the small alcove (once the floor reaches that level) and the Stranger will be safe.

Place this stone on the pedestal next to the first one, and you'll open the next door you need to enter.

There is a tricky jump in this passageway, but if you use your pistol sights to line it up, you can perform an easy running jump to make it across. Keep following the passage to the next room with a pedestal on the other side.

NOCTURNE

Don't fall into the crevices here; jump across to reach the stone. When you do, swinging blades will appear in the crevices and you'll have to time your jumps back across to miss them. Save you game, and be patient. Once you have the rhythm down, it's not difficult to make the crossing.

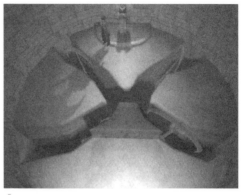

Return to Gardath's chamber and place the stone on the proper pedestal to open the next door. The first stone chamber you come to is a trap—don't grab the stone you see here. Instead, push the lever on the wall to open a secret door behind the stone. Enter the secret door and follow the path to the real stone chamber.

Once you have the stone, you've got to time your run back across to avoid a deadly mass of spikes that shoot up from the ground. Take it slow and stay in the middle of the room. Before you try, wait a few seconds and get the pattern down. Once you start moving, keep moving—it doesn't get easier if you stand there.

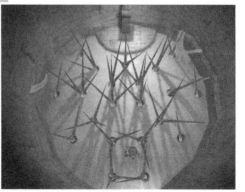

Return to Gardath's chamber and place the last stone on its pedestal. This opens the final door, allowing the Stranger to proceed across a death-defying suspension bridge to the next chamber.

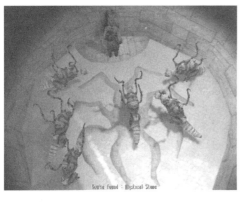

When the Stranger gets the last stone, a swarm of Drones will attack, but they won't kill him. Instead, they bind him and take him back to Gardath.

(As the Stranger is brought to the throne beneath Gardath—the Old One, the nameless priest stands for the first time.)

NOCTURNE

CHAPTER SIX: ACT TWO

Priest (to spawn):   What's wrong with you? Why didn't you kill him?

(From overhead, the earth-moving voice of the god emerges like an ancient underground river.)

Gardath: Hiator, trollor iannam. (You are being replaced.)

Priest: What? Replace me? It was I who summoned you. If not for me, you would have slept another ten millennia in this ancient pit!

Priest: I awoke you. I gave you an entire town to feed on, and this is how you repay me?

Gardath: Hiator, en gemner hotha il trae. (You no longer suit my purposes.)

Priest (gesturing at Stranger): I'm no longer useful? And this is what you choose to replace me?

Gardath: Hiacham, ju marl kron a hiator. (This human is far superior to you.)

Priest: This human is superior to me? You pathetic grub! I made you! I created you from the void you'd been banished to! If not for me, you'd-

(Gardath commands the Drones to destroy the priest. It then speaks directly to the Stranger's mind.)

Gardath: Hiator, il trae baota hough ree-ewn kiatag. (You will now take the role of my high priest.)

Stranger (grimly): The hell I will.

(The slow, rolling laughter of this eons-old god would drive men of weaker resolve insane, but the Stranger just grimaces against it.

Suddenly, from the shadowy junction to the old coal mine, Scat emerges, summoning the Baron with all his usual flash, smoke and light. He hurls bolts of lightning at the Drones, freezing them in place.)

NOCTURNE

Baron: What a mess you've gotten yourself into this time! Without my help, you'd surely die.

Stranger: Where the hell did you come from?

Baron: I see you've awoken an elder god.

Stranger: I had nothing to do with that.

Baron (laughing): I know. There's no way a little man like you could bring this monster out of eternity. But you can send it back. This entire chamber is designed to contain that monster. All you need is a binding stone. It's disc-shaped with the image of that fiend engraved on it.

Stranger (showing stone): You mean like this?

Baron: That's the one! The seal on the floor is incomplete without it. Place it in the center of the seal beneath the creature. I'll hold these foul beasts.

NOCTURNE

CHAPTER SIX: ACT TWO

There's no time to waste—quickly run to the center of the seal and place the final stone beneath Gardath. Immediately, lightning starts to send the elder god back into the void. Run back across the bridge before the Stranger gets crushed by falling debris.

Baron: You'd best get the hell out of here! Oh, and Stranger... You owe me one. The Baron laughs menacingly as the elder god's chamber disintegrates.

(The next scene shows the Stranger and Scat near the mine entrance, discussing Gardath.)

Scat: This place feels different already.

Stranger: That thing is still down there. Asleep, but still there.

Scat: Surely no one will mess with it again?

(The Stranger says nothing, but Scat gets the message.)

Scat: Yeah, right. I'll get a Spookhouse containment team out here to clean up.

(The town of Redeye is safe, and the world is safe, from a great evil — just another day for Spookhouse and the Stranger.)

NOCTURNE

NOCTURNE
Official Strategy Guide

Windy City
Massacre

Chapter Seven - Act Three

THE OFFICIAL STRATEGY GUIDE

Act 3 - Chicago - 1933

The 30s were the era of gangsters, and the mob controlled large portions of America's cities and industry. Spookhouse would ordinarily leave the mob to the Feds, but it appears that Al Capone is dabbling in something that concerns Spookhouse—re-animating dead gangsters for his diabolical purposes.

Act 3, Scene 1 – Spookhouse HQ

(The Stranger sits in the briefing room. Colonel Hapscomb stands before the projector screen.)

Colonel: There's been some peculiar activity in Chicago. Last night, one of Al Capone's hitmen, Jack "The Knife" Campelli, hit a speakeasy in East Chicago.

Stranger: Big deal. The Mob hits somebody every night these days.

Colonel: The thing is, we got a report from Elliot Ness's office two months ago that Campelli was killed in a shoot-out.

Stranger: A clerical error. Between the Feds and the Chicago cops, I'm sure names and faces get mixed up all the time.

Colonel: We don't think so. We have a new informant in Chicago: Vincenzo Gasparro. He goes by the name Icepick. He's been telling us the same thing.

NOCTURNE

CHAPTER SEVEN: ACT THREE

Colonel: Icepick saw a man who died two weeks ago gunning down members of a rival family last night.

Stranger (unbelieving): You're saying the Mafia is employing the undead now? That's ridiculous.

Colonel: Maybe not. We've learned that a German scientist named Enric Loathring immigrated to the United States three years ago. According to our intelligence, he's spent the last twenty years developing technology to raise the dead.

Stranger: Like Frankenstein? You're joking.

Colonel: I'm quite serious. If the Mafia has found a way to recycle their dead, even those who have been ripped to shreds, then it's our job to deal with it.

Stranger: Frankenstein?

Colonel: Frankenstein was fiction, Stranger. This is reality. Our own scientists are on the brink of similar technology. If we relied solely on "modern" medicine, half our operatives would be dead. Yourself included. We can revive a person who—by all known science—is dead, but even we can't do what Loathring is doing.

Colonel: If Capone's scientist has found a way to revive a man from virtually any degree of death, we're all in serious trouble.

Stranger (sarcastically): His undead army of evil will walk over the face of the earth.

Colonel (gravely): This is serious business, Stranger. What happens when the cops' bullets are useless against criminals? What happens when this savage abuse of nature spreads beyond Chicago.

Stranger (still skeptical): If you say so.

Colonel: Icepick has infiltrated Capone's gang. He'll meet you at Pier 59 in Chicago. Icepick claimed to be on the verge of discovering exactly what Capone is up to, but we've lost contact with him.

NOCTURNE

(There is a knock at the door. Colonel Hapscomb walks to the door and opens it. Standing in the doorway is General Biggs holding his hat.)

Colonel: General Biggs! Do come in.

General: I'm not too early, am I? You said to meet here at oh-nine-hundred hours.

Colonel: No, no, you're right on time, as usual. **(To Stranger)** Stranger, this is General Biggs. He will be acting as our liaison to the United States Army, so he will be popping in from time to time. Our relationship is mainly information sharing; however, if the need arises, he's the man who can get us an armed regiment to aid us.

Stranger: I thought the whole point of Spookhouse was to keep our information closely guarded.

Colonel: The General's men are fiercely loyal to him, and if they ever assist us, they will deny it to their deaths. Our secrets will not be compromised. We're all fighting for the same cause. (To Biggs) General Biggs, I would like you to meet our top operative. General Biggs, the Stranger.

General: "The Stranger" huh? You aren't hiding something that we should know, are you soldier?

Stranger: Nothing that need concern you.

CHAPTER SEVEN: ACT THREE

General: Hrm... Well, the Colonel and I go way back, so if he says something, I take his word for it. And he tells me you're the best there is. It's a pleasure meeting a man that works so hard to protect our country.

Stranger (formally, but not politely): Nice to meet you as well.

Colonel: Not to cut this short, but the General is pressed for time, and he and I need to discuss some issues. So we'll bring this meeting to a close. Watch your back, Stranger.

General: Good luck, soldier.

The mission advances when you click on the elevator at the end of the hall. Until then, you can wander about, chatting to Rogan and Svetlana. Neither of them have anything useful to offer, so entering the elevator first won't cost you anything.

Act 3, Scene 2 – Streets of Chicago (1st time)

(The Stranger enters the Pier 59 area. From the shadows, a voice calls out to him.)

Icepick: "The world is a dark place."

Stranger: You must be Icepick.

Icepick: Uh, yeah, but that ain't the password.

Stranger (frustrated at the cloak and dagger routine): Don't start with me. Spookhouse sent me. Leave it at that.

Icepick: Okay, now that we got that squared away, what should I call you?

Stranger: Stranger.

Icepick: Eh, I've heard weirder names.

(Icepick steps into the light and Stranger pulls his guns.)

Icepick: Hey, hey, hey! I thought we was jake!

NOCTURNE

Stranger: You're one of them.

Icepick: "Them" who?

Stranger: One of those re-animated monsters.

Icepick (gravely): Yeah, I was dead. That crazy German brought me back to life. You gotta problem with that?

Stranger: Yes. I make it a habit to kill monsters, not help them.

Icepick (taking offense): Hey, first off, I might look hideous, but I'm trying to stop this from happening to anyone else. I didn't ask for this. And second, you got it the wrong way around. I'm not asking for help. You need my help.

Stranger: And you didn't think you should maybe mention your condition to the Colonel?

Icepick: You guys are monster hunters. I figured no one would get sent if you knew a monster made the report. There's some freaky shit going down here, and I have information that can help you stop it. Take it or leave it.

Stranger: What have you got for me?

Icepick: There's a speakeasy down the block called the Vendome. It's behind a pet shop. Use this pass to get in.

(Icepick hands a Vendome pass to the Stranger.)

Icepick: I was supposed to meet a newspaper reporter there, but I don't exactly fit in, do I? I told him I'd send someone else in my place. He's expecting you right now. Go to the bar and order a Manhattan. My reporter friend will find you.

Icepick: Capone's ordered patrols throughout the area, so stay low as you walk around here. Stick to the alleys wherever you can.

(Icepick drifts back into the shadows. The Stranger must make his way to the Vendome.)

NOCTURNE

CHAPTER SEVEN: ACT THREE

From the shack where the Stranger meets Icepick, cross the short bridge to the docks and follow them to the left.

When you reach the street, keep moving; Capone's goons are patrolling in force, cruising the street in their cars. If you hear a car coming, look for cover. You definitely don't want to stand in the middle of the street, or you'll be run down. Gangsters will jump off and attack when they get close. When you kill a gangster, get the Tommygun he drops. Switch to it using your NEXT WEAPON key.

Follow the median down the street, and duck behind a stoop, or into an alley whenever you can. Keep following the street until it dead ends and turns right, and you see Joe's Pet Shop on the left.

NOCTURNE

THE OFFICIAL STRATEGY GUIDE

Joe's is the front for the Vendome, and the entrance is in the rear. Enter the alley beside Joe's and you'll see one of Capone's goons out back. He'll ask to see your pass, and let you enter the Vendome.

Goon: Let's see your pass.

(The Stranger slips the pass to the goon at the bottom of the stairs.)

Goon: Welcome to the Vendome.

Act 3, Scene 3 —The Vendome

(The Stranger walks upstairs and the door opens. The Vendome is a classic Prohibition era speakeasy, complete with a lounge singer and all the usual atmosphere. While the singer sings, the Stranger finds a seat at the bar.)

Stranger: Give me a Manhattan.

Bartender: A Manhattan? Big guy like you?

Stranger: Yes. (after a pause) With a Scotch chaser.

(A man approaches.)

NOCTURNE

CHAPTER SEVEN: ACT THREE

Journalist: Hello. Mind if I join you?

Stranger (never one to assume anything, including the fact that this might be the contact he is to meet): Depends.

Journalist: Icepick sent you, right? I've got information you need.

(He leads the Stranger across the room to a table.)

Journalist: A colleague of mine found out what Capone is up to in his new factory. He called it "Frankenstein's Mobsters." He went in with a camera to document it, but Capone's men found him. They took his film to the theater. Everything you need to know is on that reel. Something sinister is going on over there. I'm afraid to take the story to my editor.

(The doors bursts open, and Capone's hitmen charge in. The journalist is caught in the opening barrage. A big gunfight erupts.)

The Stranger has to make it out alive. Run to the back of the room like a little coward. You might look bad, but it's not like anyone in there is going to survive. You'll be able to pick off the mobsters one by one as they enter.

Act 3, Scene 4 – Streets of Chicago

The Stranger can't get into the theater to follow up on the journalist's tip. All doors are locked, and Capone's patrols will wipe him out if he tries. You must return to the pier and talk to Icepick again.

Make your way back down the street, using the stoops for cover to avoid Capone's hit-men. When you reach the pier, you'll find Icepick waiting behind some barrels near the bridge that leads to your original meeting place.

Icepick:	What did you find?
Stranger:	I need to get into the theater.
Icepick:	No way. That place is locked up tighter than a tomb. They still show movies there, but you've gotta be connected to get in. More connected than I am, anyway.
Icepick:	I've got a buddy in there named Mo, but he just runs the concession stand.
Stranger:	There's got to be some back way in.
Icepick:	Maybe underground. The sewer system goes under the theater, but I can't fit through the manholes.
Stranger:	How do I get into the sewers?
Icepick:	There's an entrance back here somewhere...

NOCTURNE

CHAPTER SEVEN: ACT THREE

Icepick: Here, behind this grate.

Stranger: Well done.

(He tries lifting the manhole cover.)

Stranger: I can't get a grip on this thing.

Icepick: Don't look at me. If you can't get your little fingers under it, there's no way these mitts will get in there. (gestures with big hands)

Icepick: We're gonna need a manhole key to pry it open. I think I know where to get one. The Waterworks building is on the other side of this block.

Stranger: All right, follow me.

The Waterworks isn't far from the speakeasy the Stranger just fled. Icepick will tag along, and he'll be very useful when one of Capone's men jumps out of their car to attack.

Follow the same street all the way to the end. When you get close, look for a narrow alley on the right side of the street (the Stranger's right). Duck into it and keep going straight to reach the Waterworks and avoid the street.

When the Stranger tries the door to the Waterworks, Icepick steps up and bashes it in with a few blows. Step inside to look for the manhole key.

Act 3, Scene 5 – Waterworks

(The Stranger and Icepick must find the manhole key and return to the pier.)

As soon as the Stranger enters, gunfire erupts. Return fire, and jump into the stairwell that leads below ground ahead.

This door is locked too, but Icepick will make quick work of it. Inside you'll find a cabinet against the opposite wall. Get the Doctor Bag and Manhole Key from the cabinet. Now you must retrace your steps, avoiding the gunfire above on the way out.

NOCTURNE

CHAPTER SEVEN: ACT THREE

Act 3, Scene 6 – Streets of Chicago

Once outside, use the same, narrow alley to avoid part of the street, then run back to the pier. The usual assortment of gangsters will try to run you down, or rub you out, but if you keep running, you can avoid their fire.

(Once you're back at the manhole):

Icepick: I'll have to catch up with you later. There's no way I'm squeezing into that thing.

Stranger (because he doesn't like monsters, even helpful ones): Just as well...

Icepick: I'll try to find some other way into the theater and meet you there.

(The Stranger climbs down into the sewer and heads for the theater.)

THE OFFICIAL STRATEGY GUIDE

Act 3, Scene 7 – Theater

You enter the theater in a chamber connected to the sewer, well below ground level. Climb the ladder in the next room to reach the small room above.

Get the Doctor's Bag here before continuing. Follow the narrow passageway, wiping out the goons that attack. Be sure to grab their Tommyguns when they go down, to keep the Stranger well-supplied with ammo.

Climb the ladder to the room above, and the Stranger will be backstage. A goon is headed your way, so ambush him when he comes through the curtain on the opposite side of the stage.

NOCTURNE

CHAPTER SEVEN: ACT THREE

Walk through the theater and through one of the curtains at the back. Kill the two goons on guard duty in the hallway behind the theater, then walk out to the concession stand.

(When the Stranger wanders into the foyer, the attendant at the concession stand calls out to him. He's a very excitable young hoodlum wannabe.)

Attendant: Cheezes cripes! How the hell did you get in here? I thought this place was locked up tight.

Stranger: Not tight enough. Are you Mo?

Attendant: That's me. You a friend of Icepick's?

Stranger: Yeah. He's around here somewhere.

Attendant: Hey, you've gotta see the film they got from some reporter guy. It shows all kinds of freaky stuff from inside Capone's new factory. They've got it stashed under the marquee room.

Goon (from stairs): Hey, you! What the hell!?

(Goons rush in shooting the Attendant. Fighting ensues.)

NOCTURNE

Return fire when the goon attacks. Unfortunately, Mo won't be serving any more popcorn, but he's already told you what you need to know.

Walk back into the hallway behind the concession stand and open the office door. Open the next door and kill the two Frankenmobsters inside.

In order to access the door to the room with the lever, you'll first have to find the key, which is located in the film vault room beyond the projection booth.

Push the lever across the room to open a secret door upstairs beneath the projection room. Walk up either set of stairs near the concession stand to reach the upper level of the theater. Walk up the set of stairs that are farthest from the projector, and you'll be in the back hallway.

NOCTURNE

CHAPTER SEVEN: ACT THREE

Open the closet door at the end of the hall to find a Doctor's Bag. There is another one behind the door in the center of the hallway (between the restrooms). Kill the goon in this room, then take the Doctor's Bag.

Open the door next to the closet and walk upstairs. Kill the thug on the landing above, and enter the projection room. Open the door across the room and kill the goon below. The secret door is behind the shelf of film canisters below.

Once you're in the secret room, cross to the gate in the corner and open it. The Frankenmobster film is on the floor; take it upstairs and load it onto the projector.

NOCTURNE

(As the Stranger watches the film, Smiley, the Frankenmobster boss of the theater, rips through the screen.)

Smiley: So, you're the one who busted up the Vendome. Mr. Capone don't like it when people interfere with his business.

Stranger: Who the hell are you?

Smiley: They call me Smiley. I'm Capone's clean-up man, and you're the garbage.

Smiley is immune to all of the Stranger's weapons; however, his cronies aren't. You can't leave this portion of the theater, so run between and around the seats to avoid their fire (and Smiley's deliberate attacks) as you return fire. Once they are dead, keep evading Smiley.

NOCTURNE

CHAPTER SEVEN: ACT THREE

As the Stranger evades Smiley's attacks and learns that his weapons are useless, another goon sneaks onto the balcony and starts taking pot shots at the Stranger with an elephant gun. If you can survive long enough, Icepick will sneak up behind the goon and kill him. The goon drops the gun and a crate of ammo that spills into the auditorium.

Icepick: Stranger! Grab that gun! I'll be down as quick as I can.

Get the gun and shells to attack Smiley. A few well-placed shots with the Elephant Gun and Smiley will be history.

Icepick: Great work, Stranger!

Stranger: I think you've blown your cover.

Icepick: Yeah, they were starting to get curious anyway.

Stranger: Did you see that film of Capone's factory?

NOCTURNE

THE OFFICIAL STRATEGY GUIDE

Icepick: It's a bad situation. When they brought me back, it took them weeks to stitch me together. Now it looks like they can crank out ten guys like me in a day.

Stranger: We have to stop him. Do you know where that factory is?

Icepick: North of here, I think. There's been a lot of activity up there lately.

Stranger (annoyed at having to rely on Icepick's assumption): You think? I thought you had inside information. I thought that's where they made you.

Icepick: Hey, I was just a prototype. They built me by hand in a lab across town. I've never even been inside that factory. I think there's an underground access to the warehouse that's beside the factory. I've seen people going in and out of the manhole behind this theater. It's right out here.

(Icepick kicks open the back door of the theater, then slams it shut quickly after seeing a dozen Frankenmobsters waiting to ambush.)

Icepick: Damn! They've got the place surrounded. Quick, climb up to the roof. See if you can find another way out. I'll hold these guys off.

Stranger: You're sure?

Icepick: Go!

(The Stranger mounts the ladder and Icepick kicks the door open, spilling hot lead into the back alley without hesitation. The Stranger continues up the ladder.)

There are no goons in the hallways above. Keep climbing each ladder you come to and you'll reach the walkway that runs above the backstage area. Open the door at the end of this hall, and you'll reach the roof.

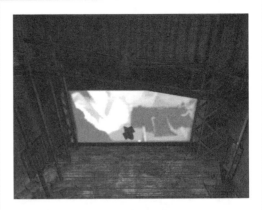

NOCTURNE

CHAPTER SEVEN: ACT THREE

Act 3, Scene 8 – Streets of Chicago

You can't make the jump from the roof you're on to the other one. Instead, climb the ladders on the water tower to reach the top. Walk along the top of the water tower, but be careful not to fall in—falling in kills the Stranger.

Push the plank that's on the corner nearest the building across the alley, and it will fall down. Drop straight down, and the Stranger will land on the plank and have an easy walk to the building roof.

Now climb down the fire escape and go to the Stranger's left. Duck into the narrow alley, and Icepick will meet you there.

NOCTURNE

Icepick: Hey, look what I found. It's a flame-thrower. You'll have to find some fuel for it, though. The rejuvenation chemicals they use are extremely flammable. Those freaks will go up like Roman candles with this thing. If you really want to screw Capone's game, hit a few of the chemical canisters at his warehouse with this and watch it blow. You can level the whole goddamn place.

Stranger: You coming along?

Icepick: Are you kidding? I'm just as flammable as the rest of those monsters. I'm not going to be anywhere near that place when you blow it up.

Stranger (impressed): Your assistance has been quite useful.

Icepick: You know, you aren't the friendliest guy I've met, but you're all right, Stranger. Before I died, I worked with some guys I thought I trusted. I won't make that mistake again. Even though you don't like me, I've got the feeling that I can trust you.

Icepick: I'm glad we can put a stop to Capone's deranged plan to make more monsters like me. I wouldn't wish this on anyone.

(The Stranger pauses silently before rushing to the manhole and diving into the dark depths.)

NOCTURNE

CHAPTER SEVEN: ACT THREE

Act 3, Scene 9 – Warehouse

> NOTE: The warehouse is full of explosive material, from boxes crammed on shelves, to barrels of flammable liquid. Be sure that you keep on the move during a fire fight to avoid an untimely death from an explosion.

From the Stranger's starting point inside the warehouse, turn to his right and hug the wall. As you pass the shelves ahead, you'll see a guard shack. A thug will open fire from inside the shack; light him up with the Flamethrower. Step inside the shack and get the fuel, Doctor's Bag, and battery, then retrace your steps toward your entry point.

In the corner you'll find some wooden stairs. Walk upstairs and kill the goon above. Grab the Flamethrower fuel he had on him, and go back downstairs. Make your way through the warehouse, and take down the goons that are guarding the area. There are flammable boxes on virtually every shelf, so be cautious about using the Flamethrower indiscriminately— an exploding box will inflict serious damage on the Stranger.

NOCTURNE

153

Look for a ladder near a chain-link fence and climb up. Get to the other end of this hallway quickly, and kill the thug firing at you. If the Stranger gets caught near the ladder, the thug will shoot the explosive barrels and kill him. Either way, the barrels will explode, blocking this as a route back.

Walk down the stairs and hug the wall beneath them. A truck is parked ahead; wax the goon who is patrolling here and walk around to the front of the truck.

Enter the restroom and get the Flamethrower fuel inside. There are three more canisters in the office next door, but they are guarded by a good. Let him have it and grab the fuel. Go through the other door of the restroom and kill the goon just outside. The cannisters in the bathroom will explode, blocking your way back.

NOCTURNE

CHAPTER SEVEN: ACT THREE

Keep exploring the warehouse; near the truck ahead, two goons will ambush you. Use the Flamethrower, but keep the Stranger away from them as they burn— if the fire spreads to the Stranger, it's over.

Just past the truck is another stairway; kill the thug below it, but don't bother going upstairs. Keep following the path, and turn left when you come to a dead end. When you reach the long hallway with tables in it, get the Doctor's Bag and fuel from the first table, then go through the doorway on the left at the end of the hall.

Kill the three goons back here, then climb the stairs. Follow the catwalk above and walk across the gap in the chain link fence. Drop down below to reach the area behind the first guard-house you saw.

NOCTURNE

Smiley, re-animated once again (but with some new appendages), will burst through the office wall ahead. Use the Flamethrower on him, and keep backing up to avoid his attack. Once he's history (again), enter the office.

Act 3, Scene 10 – Factory

This segment of the Stranger's mission is short and sweet—make it through this portion of the factory to stop Capone's Frankenstein machine.

Kill the thug that drops down from above, then climb the stairs ahead. Kill the goons on the platform around the chemical vat, then head down the stairs on the other side.

CHAPTER SEVEN: ACT THREE

There are two goons waiting for you there, so don't get caught in their cross-fire. Run past them if you need more breathing room.

Cross the machine room and head for the upper right corner of the room. Along the way, you'll face several more Frankenmobsters; rub 'em out, then turn the corner near the conveyor belt nearest the wall.

Open the door ahead to enter the next part of the factory.

THE OFFICIAL STRATEGY GUIDE

Act 3, Scene 11 - Factory

This section of the factory is anything but deserted—it's crawling with goons. You start on a catwalk and as you follow it around, several goons will try to stop you. Keep following the walkway and get to ground level. Here you'll find the Main Valve (behind the chemical vat). Kill the goons near it, then push the lever in front of it to close the valve.

Go back upstairs and follow the walkway to the other end, where there is another lever. Push the lever to start a chain reaction explosion. Get your pistols out, and get out of there! As you turn to leave, what's left of Smiley will drop down from above, wrecking the walkway.

Stranger: I see you're not smiling anymore.

Smiley: This time, you die!

Unfortunately for Smiley, you can bring him down with one well-placed shot. Note that your pistols are aimed (if you are using auto-aim) at a point above Smiley. Fire at the catwalk support, and Smiley will be dumped into the vat of chemicals, where he burns up as the Stranger steps to safety.

It seems that Smiley was wrong. He dies, again, and for the last time.

NOCTURNE

NOCTURNE
Official Strategy Guide

The House on the
Edge of Hell

Chapter Eight – Act Four

Act 4 - France - 1935

Hamilton Killian, a former Spookhouse operative who left prior to the Stranger's appearance, has asked for some assistance with an undead problem at his estate. The Stranger has been dispatched to provide whatever help is necessary.

Act 4, Scene 1 – Spookhouse HQ

(The Stranger enters HQ alone and stands before the secretary in the proxy office without saying anything.)

Stranger (eventually): This is ridiculous.

Secretary: Everyone has to say the password, Stranger. Even you.

Stranger: An intruder would be dead by now.

Secretary: Rules, Stranger. You think I enjoy sitting in this little box all day?

Stranger: Your enjoyment does not concern me.

Secretary: The password, Stranger.

Stranger: By this point I could have killed you and flipped the switch to open the door myself.

Secretary (laughing): You wouldn't do that.

Secretary (not so sure): Would you?

Stranger (after a disturbingly long pause and an angry sigh): "The world is a dark place."

Secretary: "Who will protect the world from darkness?"

Stranger: "We will." ... After we play our stupid games.

CHAPTER EIGHT: ACT FOUR

(Secretary activates the secret door.)

Secretary: Have a nice day.

Stranger: What's left of it...

(The Stranger makes his way to the secret HQ where Colonel Hapscomb meets him. Svetlana and Icepick talk in the corner. Haystack trains in the gym.)

Colonel: Ah, Stranger. I have a somewhat... personal request.

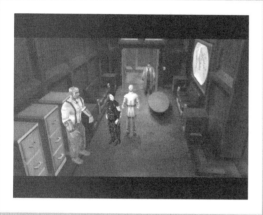

The Colonel leads the Stranger to the briefing room. You can follow him immediately, or chat with Svetlana and Icepick. Neither of them know anything about the Colonel's request, so you'll need to enter the briefing room eventually.

(When the Stranger enters the briefing room, General Biggs is already there.)

General: Greetings, soldier.

Stranger: General Biggs.

General: I see you two have a mission to discuss, so I will take my leave, now. It was good to see you again, Hapscomb.

General (as he passes the Stranger, he salutes farewell): Stranger.

Colonel: Do you have time after this briefing, perhaps?

General: No. Unfortunately, I have a meeting at thirteen-hundred hours in Pennsylvania.

THE OFFICIAL STRATEGY GUIDE

Colonel: Just as well, I have an immense amount of paperwork to attend to.

General: I know what you mean.

Colonel: Thanks for stopping by, General; it is always a pleasure to speak with you.

General: Good bye, Colonel. Good luck on your mission, soldier.

(After the General exits):

Colonel: Do you remember Hamilton Killian?

Stranger: He was an operative just before I came to Spookhouse.

Colonel: That's right. He served Spookhouse from 1909 to 1922. He's retired now, living in France. He contacted me recently requesting help. He says that a graveyard near his estate outside of Paris has been disturbed by supernatural activity.

Stranger: Killian was supposedly the best in his day. What could possibly be a problem for him?

Colonel: He didn't offer much detail in his letter, but apparently the phenomena occurring there are is more than even he can handle. He has requested that I send Spookhouse's best monster-hunter.

Stranger (not really a question): Me.

Colonel: Who else?

You once again have control of the Stranger. While you can leave for the mission at any time, be sure to talk to Svetlana and Icepick to gain some more insight into Killian. Also, Doc Holliday, who was at Spookhouse when Killian was still an operative, has some very valuable information about Killian.

Doc Holliday is in the lab. To get her to talk, the Stranger will have to keep pestering her, but she knows:

NOCTURNE

CHAPTER EIGHT: ACT FOUR

Holliday: Not now, Stranger, I'm busy.

Stranger: I need some items for the undead or demons.

Holliday: Does it mean nothing to you when I tell you I'm busy?

Holliday (exasperated sigh): Okay, what kind of undead? Zombies? Vampires? What?

Stranger: Unsure, maybe zombies.

(Holliday peruses the items on her workbench.)

Holliday: Well, I have this for Type One zombies, but if they're any other kind of zombie, you're out of luck. And for demons I have some of this. But I don't think you want to carry the eighty-pound canister with you, do you?

Stranger: No thanks.

Stranger: The mission is a request of Hamilton Killian.

Holliday: Killian? Oh God! I knew him. I came to Spookhouse just before he left. He was... scary. The most bitter man I've ever known. I think he was already insane by the time I met him. I'm sure you've heard all the stories.

Stranger: I've heard a lot of stories. I'd like to know the facts. Since you were here, maybe you can set the record straight.

Holliday proceeds to tell the Stranger all about Killian. Be sure to keep her talking, as she is the only Spookhouse operative who knew Killian prior to his breakdown and subsequent retirement. You'll know that Holliday has said all she knows when she keeps repeating that she's busy. It's important that you hear it all before going on your mission.

Get the Doctor's Bag and Ax from her workbench, then get the Shotgun and ammo from near the door. Enter the elevator to begin the mission.

NOCTURNE

Act 4, Scene 2 – Killian's Estate

(Outside Killian's mansion.)

Killian: Welcome to my home. I'm glad I can still rely on my old friends at Spookhouse. My name is Hamilton Killian. I hear I'm to call you "Stranger."

Stranger: Yes. Colonel Hapscomb speaks highly of you.

Killian: It's nice to know that I am remembered. The Colonel is a good man.

Stranger: So what's the situation?

Killian: A couple of months ago, one of my groundskeepers disappeared without a trace. While searching the grounds, I found that some of the corpses in the nearby graveyard had risen. And smaller imp-like demons were running rampant. I took those creatures down, but a couple of nights later, they returned. And their numbers had increased. I returned periodically to keep them in check. To my dismay, they began regenerating faster and faster.

Killian: To be honest, going out night after night to deal with them was more of a nuisance than anything else. But now there are so many monsters that I fear for my property and my safety. As I said, I can take them down, but they just keep coming back...you might say I'm at my wit's end. I hate to have this incident sully my image, but I gave up my grandiose monster-hunting days long ago. The Colonel assures me that you are just the man to take care of my little... problem.

Stranger: It won't be a problem for long.

Killian: Splendid, old chap. I trust you will not be needing my assistance. I will remain here. Just follow this path, and it will take you to the graveyard. Happy hunting.

NOCTURNE

CHAPTER EIGHT: ACT FOUR

The Stranger goes to the graveyard. Kill any Imps you see, but think twice about killing skeletons. Killing skeletons causes them to regenerate faster. Also, Imps will continue to attack even without heads, so be sure they are dead before you turn your back on them.

Several Imps and some skeletons will ambush you shortly after you enter the graveyard. Search the Imp bodies—they have three keys you need. The skeletons are not much of a threat, but each time you kill them, they regenerate faster. You can usually outrun them, which is the best way to deal with them—they become inert and just stand there if you're not in range.

Each key opens one of the crypts near the entrance to the cemetery. Once you've collected all three keys, begin opening the crypts. Inside the one on your left, the Stranger notices that something is missing from the pillar inside. He will also note, if you look at the symbol on the floor, that the same kind of cross is on some of the monuments in the cemetery.

In the crypt on the right as you enter the cemetery, he'll make the same observations. Note that the shape of the missing cross is different here. You need to find the crosses that go in the two crypts.

NOCTURNE

If you assume that the central crypt is North, then the cross for the East crypt is on top of a tomb just South of it. Climb up and take the ankh-shaped cross from the top of the tomb.

Place the cross in the East crypt, and the shadow will fill the symbol on the floor. Cross the cemetery to the West crypt. You'll notice that there is no light shining inside this crypt—something on the roof is blocking it.

Climb the ivy on the side of the crypt to reach the roof. The Stranger can toss the ivy on top over the side, and light will shine down into the crypt. Climb down and get the cross from the first tomb on your right as you enter the cemetery.

NOCTURNE

CHAPTER EIGHT: ACT FOUR

Place the cross in the crypt, and three altars labelled Water, Flame, and Wind will rise from the center of the cemetery. Walk up the steps of the center crypt.

Two gargoyles will attack from the front of the center crypt as the Stranger opens the door. Kill them and step inside. The Stranger discovers a witch's staff inside this crypt, which is the source of the problem. You can't destroy it by shooting it, so step behind it and open the crypt to reveal a downward passage. Follow the passage underground.

You'll see several pillars topped by symbols, as well as a lever next to an inscription on the wall. The inscription reads:

With the light, cut the night.

You need to push the proper pillars so that the shadow matches the inscription on the wall. The proper pillars are the first and third, moving away from the inscription. Once the pillars are in place, push the lever near the inscription, and three doors will open along the wall.

The three vessels inside each have different contents: water, air, flame. Also, he finds an inscription on the wall to the right of the alcoves:

Fire and Water and Air of dark worth
In a room far beneath the earth,
Find the marble tomb of birth
To an altar surrounded by graves,
The destination of the three is paved
Forsee all of air consumed by hellish fire
And the liquid that will douse the funeral pyre
Behold, leaving water with air is the only desire
If one destroyed, of those that remain
Replace to origin and resurrect again.

The Stranger must solve the puzzle and get all three vessels to the three altars above ground.

To do so:

1. Take the Fire vessel from the mausoleum room first, and put it in the Flame slot of the altar upstairs.

2. Go back underground, and take Water or Air to the altar and place it in its proper slot.

3. Take the Fire vessel from the altar, and bring it back to the mausoleum room.

4. Now take whichever vessel was left underground in step 2 (either Water or Air) to the altar.

5. Finally, go back and get the Fire vessel and bring it to the altar with the other vessels. All three are together in the center.

Rules of the Element puzzle:

1. If you put down a vessel anywhere other than the center or mausoleum room altars, the vessel will explode in a couple of seconds like dynamite. It will then regenerate (if the Stranger didn't die in the explosion) in the mausoleum room, resetting the puzzle to an extent. This will also allow you to use a vessel as a weapon, mainly against the imps. You will have to return any vessels already placed upstairs to their original alcoves in order to try again.

NOCTURNE

CHAPTER EIGHT: ACT FOUR

2. *If you take a vessel that leaves a predatory vessel with its prey, the prey will begin magically disappearing, totally dissipating in a few moments (the Stranger needs time to pick it up before it disappears). For the vessels to reappear, the player must return all remaining vessels to the mausoleum room. They will then all regenerate, resetting the puzzle. For example, you take Fire and place it in it's center altar. You must take Water and leave. Water will make Fire disappear. You must replace Water in the underground mausoleum room to regenerate Fire.*

Once the Stranger has solved the puzzle and placed the final vessel on the altar, it shoots bolts of lightning at the North Mausoleum, causing the witch's staff to explode. This creates a chain reaction of skeletons blowing up. Once they are all destroyed, the Stranger begins to exit.

Stranger: Black magic. Killian knows black magic. His little "monster problem" reeks of foul play. I think it's time to have a little chat with the "old chap."

(The Stranger walks into the mansion. At the front porch):

Killian: Well done, Stranger!

Stranger: Skip the bullshit, Killian. What's your game?

Killian: I'm afraid I don't follow.

Stranger: That was black magic raising those monsters. The same kind of magic you studied at Spookhouse.

(Killian walks toward the door. The Stranger follows.)

Killian: Very clever, Stranger. You will be a most worthy subject.

Stranger: What is that supposed to mean?

(Killian stuns the Stranger.)

Killian (to himself happily): Very worthy, indeed.

Act 4, Scene 3 – Killian's Mansion

Recovering from Killian's blow, the Stranger stands and shakes his head to clear it. In the room are some dead bodies, and a Werewolf chained to the wall.

Avoid the Werewolf and get the amulet from the bones nearby. As the Stranger picks it up, he realizes it is Moloch's amulet.

Stranger: So this was Moloch's fate.

The wall on the far side of the Werewolf will slide back, giving the Stranger access to the next area.

As the Stranger walks down the hall, a zombie will drop from the ceiling. Keep going—it will injure itself in the fall and you're much faster than it, even when it was uninjured.

Do not walk into the center of the next room. Likewise, don't grab a weapon from the statue in the corner. Either will result in a quick death for the Stranger. Instead, open the closed door for some quick entertainment—this room is full of zombies that are just standing around. When they see the Stranger, they'll come toward him. So will the two massive gattling guns in the room. Back out, and the guns will slaughter all the zombies.

CHAPTER EIGHT: ACT FOUR

The open door is a trap. Stand in the doorway and watch the hapless zombie across the room fry himself on the electrified floor tiles. To get across, The Stranger must not touch any 'hot' tiles. The "Os" in the diagram below show the safe tiles (you'll need to jump over the black tile to the left of the first tile in the room, but after that, it's just a matter of following the safe tiles.

Tile Diagram (safe tiles are marked with 0)

```
        X     X     X     X     X
        X     X     X     X     0  ←
        X     X     X     X     X
        X     X     X     X     0
        X     X     X     0     0
  ←     X     X     X     0     X
        0     0     0     0     X
```

The next area is a long hallway with multiple doors. Most of the doors open on blank walls, but at least one will let the Stranger access an elevator. Before walking down the hall, walk up to the first door on the right. Look right, and flip the switch that is second from the left.

Now head down the hall and dodge the zombies until you can enter the only door that opens—it's two to the left of the one with carpet in front of it. Push the elevator button three times, then make a running leap across the empty shaft to the hallway on the other side.

The only door that's useful is the last one on the right, but to get there, you must evade the zombie hiding behind the tapestry ahead. The floor of the small bathroom you fall into has a Doctor's Bag on it.

Cross the hall outside the bathroom and turn left. None of the doors here are open, but follow the hallway left of the elevator. The last door before the bookcase at the dead end is the Library. Enter, and Killian will taunt the Stranger.

(In the Library, Killian calls from an intercom overhead):

Killian (over intercom): Congratulations, Stranger. You're doing fairly well, so far. I hope my traps are to your liking. What do you think of me now, Stranger? Am I crazy? No, I'm not crazy! I'm not the one who works alongside monsters. Did it anger you to find your fellow operative's emaciated corpse? Were you enraged, monster-lover, to find nothing left but a corpse? I made this place to kill and torture monsters because they deserve no less.

NOCTURNE

CHAPTER EIGHT: ACT FOUR

Stranger (under his breath, disbelieving Killian's misjudgment of his affinity for monsters): Monster lover?

Killian: And you are here because you are no better. You are here to die, Stranger. Know whom I admire, Stranger? Harry Houdini. An unparalleled master of escape. Would that I could put him through my maze... If you hope to ever escape alive, I suggest you look him up.

If you search the wrong shelves in the Library, a Werewolf will crash through the bookcases shortly after Killian is done speaking; run out the Library door and return to the elevator.

Follow the hall to the right of the elevator and push the picture of Houdini on the wall to open a secret door. Follow the passage to the right—looking through the peepholes in the wall will reveal a woman bound to a bed inside one of the rooms. Keep going and open the door at the end of the hall.

Leap over the carpeted stairs—they are a trap—and enter the Music Room. Here, Killian will taunt the Stranger further.

NOCTURNE

173

THE OFFICIAL STRATEGY GUIDE

Killian: Hello, Stranger. Welcome to my music room. This is one of my most beloved rooms. I am a man of culture. I find books and music exhilarating. There's a hint for you. Many times, books and music go hand in hand.

Killian: I'm keeping tabs on our little game. I have sensors attached to every doorway in this mansion. I know when you enter and when you leave. You know, you're much closer to me than you probably imagine. I'm directly below you in the ballroom. Come and get me now, if you like, though I wouldn't recommend it. In the meantime, I'll be down here watching as you pick up that book.

*Get the book, The **Game of Chess**, from the center of the room (If you play the victrola, you'll hear the not-so-soothing sounds of the Werewolf Symphony.), return to the Library and take a look at the chessboard. The pieces form an arrow pointing to one of the shelves. Search that shelf and you'll find a book titled **The Werewolf Symphony**. Getting it opens a secret passage behind the bookshelves. Enter and go down the spiral staircase.*

You can just make out a servant's key laying on the ground behind the spiral staircase. Get it and return to the hall in front of the Houdini portrait.

NOCTURNE

CHAPTER EIGHT: ACT FOUR

Use the key on the door to the Stranger's left and enter the pantry. Use the dumbwaiter behind the wooden doors to access the basement level (the first floor down has bars across the entrance). If you use the dumbwaiter to go up, you'll find yourself in a room that attaches to the hallway you were in near the elevator upstairs.

Once in the basement, follow the hallway through the wooden door frame and walk into the crusher chamber. Get the Warden Key near the spike pit, then enter the torture chamber. Get the Doctor's Bag on the guillotine, and the Bedroom Key from the floor in front of the cot. Use the dumbwaiter to go back upstairs.

Enter the bedroom in front of the elevator. A Succubus is chained to the bed, and she begs the Stranger to come closer. If you do, Stranger will free her and she will attack. Instead, turn off the light.

Succubus (angrily): What are you doing? You can't see me with the lights off!

Stranger: That's the point. I don't have time for your distractions, succubus.

Take the control panel from the dresser, and leave the bedroom. Use the control panel on the elevator in the hall, then leap across to reach the lounge on the other side.

Take the Shotgun and Crossbow from the wall beyond the pool table, then get the shells and bullets from the chests beneath them. The door near the guns leads back into the hall. Instead of opening it, push the large bookcase near the wall, and it will move aside to reveal another elevator.

Entering the elevator won't take you anywhere, and if you push the wrong lever, you'll be burned to a crisp. Pressing the lever nearest to the door releases a Werewolf directly behind the Stranger, so be prepared to blast it when it pounces. Inside, the Werewolf's cage is locked, but the Warden Key you have will open it. Enter the cell and climb down the ladder inside.

You'll find yourself inside another pantry. Open the door here and you'll be inside the kitchen. Some Ghouls will attack, so blast them into shreds and get the Doctor's Bag from the counter. Open the gate blocking the dumbwaiter, so you can use it later. Enter the open doorway (the other doors lead out into the hall).

NOCTURNE

CHAPTER EIGHT: ACT FOUR

Don't walk on the rugs in the dining hall—trapdoors will open, dropping the Stranger into the crushers below. To reach the other side, walk along the table instead.

The next room is the ballroom, where the Stranger will have to fight off three Werewolves. Killian isn't here anymore, so search the fireplace for the Clockroom Key, then climb back up the shelves in the pantry to return to the second floor.

Use the dumb waiter to go up to the third floor, and enter the hallway outside the room where you arrive. Open the first door on the left with your new key and enter the circular room behind it.

This is a light beam puzzle laid out in the shape of a clock. Your goal is to open the door at 12 o'clock by getting the red and blue light beams to shine equally on the purple gem beneath the door (in effect, creating purple light) to open it. Gems can only be moved by their color of light beam.

Walk to the center of the room and use the mirror there to aim the movable red beam of light at the gem sitting at the base of the door at 7 o'clock. This will move the red gem to 6 o'clock. Now use the blue beam to move the blue gem at 8 o'clock to 7 o'clock. Don't hold the beams in place after the gems move, or they'll move back—move the beams slightly aside once the gems are in place.

THE OFFICIAL STRATEGY GUIDE

Now move the gem at 2 o'clock to 3 o'clock, the gem at 9 o'cloclk to 8 o'clock, 10 o'clock to 9 o'clock, 1 o'clock to 2 o'clock, and finally 11 o'clock to 10 o'clock. This will raise two more mirrors near the purple gem. Balance the two beams of light—red and blue—until the light shining on the gem at 12 o'clock is purple. This will open the door.

Killian: Splendid! I love having a test subject who can stand up to not only the physical rigors, but also the intellectual challenge, of my maze. You've done well so far. But here's a trap that will require both body and mind to solve. Enjoy!

This is the crusher room, and you'll have to move fast to scale the wall before the Stranger gets crushed. Push the lever on the wall across from the moving wall to push the first step out. Step up onto it and push the lever on the right, then step up again. Run across and push the one on the left. Finally, push the last lever on the right to reach the top and safety. Follow the stairs down to the next challenge.

The next room is the deadliest yet—jets of flame shoot from the floor. One touch of the flames, and the Stranger will be burned to a crisp. Watch the flames for awhile until you see a pattern, then leap across the shortest part of the trap—the trap nearest the wall on your right

NOCTURNE

CHAPTER EIGHT: ACT FOUR

The Demon Key on the floor is sitting on a trapdoor. To trigger it without falling in, pick up a piece of the dismembered corpse nearby and toss it onto the trapdoor. They key will fall into the ballroom below. Enter the next room and get the Dungeon Key from the corner of the room, then have the Stranger push the rug aside to reveal a hatch you can climb down through—don't jump—the left side of the hatch has a ladder you can use.

You need to get to the ballroom, but also to the basement level. The dumb waiter is on the third floor where you left it, so you'll need to go get it in order to get to the basement. To get the dumbwaiter, you first need to go down the main stairway to the ballroom and collect the Demon Key from the ballroom floor. Once you have it, walk back upstairs and follow the hall past the Library until you come to a set of short steps leading up.

Step out onto the ledge and climb up the ladder. When you reach the hall above, open the secret door on the right, then turn left. Keep following the hall, and when you reach the hall with multiple doors, open the last one on the Stranger's left. Keep going and you'll end up in the hallway near the one with electrocuting tiles—very near the beginning of the Stranger's ordeal.

Open the elevator door you used before, and leap across the shaft. You now have the key for the third door on the left, so use it to open a room with a pentagram on the floor. Beware—stepping into the circle of the pentagram summons a fiery demon. Quickly step in and then out, and blast the demon that appears before the Stranger catches on fire. Once the demon is dead, get the box of matches on the floor.

The dumbwaiter is in the room at the end of the next hallway; take it all the way down to the basement level and enter the torture chamber. Open the dungeon door that was previously locked, and push the first lever on the Stranger's left as you enter.

This opens an empty cell. Close examination of the back wall reveals that it has been hastily bricked over. Push it, and the Stranger will break it down. Moloch is imprisoned in the chamber beyond.

Moloch (weak but enthusiastic): Stranger?

Stranger: Moloch?

Moloch: I thought I would rot here for decades before seeing another Spookhouse agent.

Stranger: There was a corpse in the cell upstairs. It looked like you.

Moloch (proudly): It was my doppelganger. Killian intercepted me on my way

to Strasbourg and threw me into this little rat-maze of his. I concocted a double of myself to use as a decoy. I nearly escaped, but he caught me and dropped me into this icy pit.

NOCTURNE

CHAPTER EIGHT: ACT FOUR

Stranger: Why hasn't he killed you?

Moloch: Ha! That is beyond his power. How can he kill someone who has been expelled from both Heaven and Hell? He took full advantage of my immortality. He gets perverse joy from putting me through this rat maze. I'm his first test subject that can't be completely killed by his traps. I've been through this maze  seventeen times. Twice I've almost escaped. Once I was within reach of the villain himself, and had I more strength, I would have eviscerated him on the spot.

Moloch: Stranger, you must free me. With my help, you can escape this place, and I can exact my revenge on that villain. Break the circle that contains me.

(Break the seal to free Moloch.)

Stranger: Accept my help, not as a personal favor, but as an obligation to Spookhouse.

Moloch: Ahh! Thank you, Stranger. Already I can feel my strength returning. But the cold here is unbearable. Killian knows that I take my strength from heat and fire. Find some means by which my dark soul can be warmed.

Moloch can't follow Stranger up the dumbwaiter, so you need to find a heat source here. Fortunately, there's a gridiron in the torture chamber. Light it with the matches you found upstairs, and Moloch will leap onto it.

Moloch: Ahh, yes! I have needed this for a long time. And now there is just one final thing I need to fully regain my strength.

Moloch (seemingly threatening the Stranger): While this fire fuels me, I need the energy found only in living blood...

Stranger (definitely threatening): Try it, and I'll finish what Killian started.

Moloch (chuckles): No, not you. I doubt your little body would begin to satisfy my thirst. There are creatures throughout this mansion. Have you seen any nearby?

Lead Moloch to the crocodile pit, and he'll feast on the creatures there.

Moloch (laughing): Yes! You've saved us both, Stranger. I am at full strength. Meet me in Killian's control room on the third floor. The day of reckoning has arrived for Hamilton Killian.

CHAPTER EIGHT: ACT FOUR

With a leap, Moloch rockets upward through the elevator shaft, crashing through the house above.

To reach the control room, take the dumbwaiter back upstairs and cross over to the hallway on the right. Open the door that is second from the end on the left, and push the lever inside. Climb the ladder inside to reach the control room.

Tip: The room with the turret guns provides an excellent supply of body parts you can use to trigger the electric floor puzzle in the next room.

Tip: Moloch's amulet fits perfectly in the statue holding the weapons. Once you've placed it there, you are free to take the weapon of your choice. The smaller ax can be stored in the Stranger's overcoat but requires closer attacks than the long spear.

NOCTURNE

THE OFFICIAL STRATEGY GUIDE

(In the control room, Moloch clutches Killian in one massive clawed fist.)

Killian: Stranger! You made it! Thank god! Help me! Get this fiend off me!

Moloch: If there's anything you want to say to this man, Stranger, say it now. He's on his way to a hell worse than the one that spawned me.

(The Stranger turns to leave, having nothing to say.)

Killian: Stranger? Wait, come back! Aren't you going to help me?

(The Stranger continues to walk away.)

Stranger: No.

(As the Stranger walks away, around the corner, the sounds of Moloch's delighted evisceration of Killian echoes loudly throughout the mansion.)

NOCTURNE

NOCTURNE
Official Strategy Guide

Chapter Nine - Epilogue

Act 5 - Nevada - 1947

Act 5, Scene 1 - Spookhouse HQ

The Stranger exits the elevator in the government building and walks down the hallway. The door to the Biological and Wildlife Research Labratory is already open. Upon entering, the Stranger sees the secretary is gone. Her chair is overturned and a couple of drops of blood are on her white desk pad.

Stranger: Something's wrong.

(Upon examination of the desk):

Stranger: Blood on the desk.

Activate the switch, opening the panel. All hall lights are off except the one red light above the elevator. Open the elevator door and descend to Spookhouse HQ.

NOCTURNE

CHAPTER NINE: EPILOGUE

All lights are out in the hall with the team portrait. When Stranger enters the Spookhouse offices, he sees that the whole place is trashed and devoid of people. A tiny bit of light coming from under the closed briefing room door, and a couple of desk lamps knocked to the floor and partially covered by office debris, are the only lights. Body parts and blood are everywhere. The filing cabinets are opened and their contents dumped on the floor. Files are strewn everywhere.

Stranger: What the hell happened? Someone's been going through all the personnel and mission files.

Trying the briefing room door reveals that it's locked.

Stranger: Locked. Doc Holliday keeps a spare set of keys in the lab.

Go into the lab to get the keys from the counter. The tables are gone; body parts and instruments litter the floor. The only light in the lab is coming from the smoking, flashing computer on fire.

Upon entering:

Stranger (solemnly): No signs of life. No sign of Holliday. **(after getting keys)** Holliday's spare keys. One of these will open the Briefing Room door.

The Stranger enters the briefing room.

(From here on, you have no control. The Stranger enters the briefing room, which is a scene of total carnage. On the screen, scrawled in someone's blood is the message):

Finally found you, Stranger.

(As the scene fades, the Stranger's gaze takes in the message, and it's clear that he knows who left it. He turns to leave the briefing room, intent on revenge...but that's a tale for another time.)

Fade Out.